40 CLASSIC WALKS
IN
THE BRECON BEACONS
NATIONAL PARK

Chris Barber

Originally published in 1997 as
Classic Walks in the Brecon Beacons National Park

This much revised edition published in 2009

Blorenge Cottage, Church Lane, Llanfoist,
Abergavenny, Gwent NP7 9NG
Tel: 01873 856114

Printed by MWL Print Group Ltd,
Units 10-13, Pontyfelin Industrial Estate,
Pontypool, Gwent NP4 ODG
Tel: 01495 750033

Front Cover Picture: *Below the North East face of Pen y Fan* – Anne Marie Barber
Back Cover Picture: *Sgwd Isaf Clungwyn on the River Mellte* – Chris Barber

DEDICATION

In memory of my good friends: John Sansom, a stalwart member of the Brecon Beacons Park Society and John Inns of Crickhowell Adventure Gear, who both did so much to help people enjoy exploring this wonderful area.

CONTENTS

'When we reach the mountain summits we leave behind us all the things that weigh heavily down below on our body and our spirit. We leave behind all sense of weakness and depression; we find a new freedom, a great exhilaration, an exhaltation of the body no less than of the spirit. We feel a great joy.'

J. C. Smutts

ACKNOWLEDGEMENTS

I am grateful to numerous friends who have given assistance in the preparation of this book. It has certainly been a labour of love for I have thoroughly enjoyed all the walks undertaken during many years of research. Some of these routes have been shared with my wife Anne and fellow members of the Gwent Mountaineering Club. Special thanks are also due to Nick Kingsford for drawing the maps.

On the summit of Pen y Fan at sunset

IMPORTANT

Whilst every effort has been made to ensure that the information in this book is correct, the author or the publisher can accept no responsibility for errors, loss or injury however caused. Your use of this book indicates your assumption of the risks involved in mountain walking and is an acknowledgement of your own sole responsibility for your safety.

FOREWORD

In my capacity as President of the National Parks Council I visited the Brecon Beacons National Park on several occasions and have two memories of walking with Chris Barber, who impressed me with his enthusiasm and extensive knowledge of this very beautiful part of Wales.

On the first occasion we enjoyed a ridge walk from Capel-y-ffin to Llanthony, taking in Chwarel y Fan, which Chris informed me was the highest point in Gwent. The views were superb on that clear but windy day and I particularly remember the bird's eye view of Llanthony Priory nestling in the Vale of Ewyas.

Five years later, on a return visit, blessed by a lovely July day, Chris guided us around some of the spectacular waterfalls in the vicinity of Ystradfellte and once again his wealth of Knowledge added greatly to our enjoyment of this remarkable series of wooded and craggy valleys, which have become known as the 'Waterfall Country'.

Standing behind the cascading curtain of Sgwd yr Eira ('Spout of Snow') on the Afon Hepste, was an experience I shall long remember and I hope one day to find time to complete Chris Barber's route which he has named 'The Waterfall Roundabout', visiting all the falls on a circular walk.

My overall impression of the Brecon Beacons National Park is the attraction of its rich variety of Scenery and as one of the less crowded of the Parks it provides truly delightful walking country for those who love wild places. Chris Barber's new edition of *Classic Walks in the Brecon Beacons National Park* is an ideal guidebook for those who wish to explore the Park and find out more about this fascinating area.

Sir Chris Bonington

'See in the distance swelling to the skies,
Like giant twins the lofty Beacons rise,
While lesser hills eastward and westward roll,
And form a beautious and harmonious whole.'

Richard Hall
Local Poet

Pen y Fan and Corn Du from Mynydd Illtud

INTRODUCTION

The Brecon Beacons National Park was established in 1957 under the provision of the National Parks and Access to the Countryside Act of 1949. This was the third National Park to be established in Wales, and it covers an area of 515 square miles, almost half of which is common land which mean that walkers may enjoy access to a wide expanse of open country.

Although the Park takes its name from the Brecon Beacons, there are in fact four ranges of mountains in the area and several isolated peaks as well. In compiling this guide I have divided the Park into areas of specific interest: Black Mountains, Three Peaks of Abergavenny, Mynydd Llangattwg & Mynydd Llangorse, Brecon Beacons, Waterfall Country, Fforest Fawr and the Carmarthen Fans.

Rising high in the Carmarthen Fans, on a rib of ground between the twin lakes of Llyn y Fan Fawr and Llyn y Fan Fach, is the River Usk which forms the main artery of the Park. Its tributaries branch off like veins on either side.

Natural lakes in the Park include the tiny Llyn cwm Llwch at 570 metres (nearly 2,000 ft) above sea level, below the forbidding slopes of Corn Du, and Llyn Safadan, otherwise known as Llangorse Lake. This is the largest natural lake in South Wales. In addition there are numerous reservoirs which were built in Victorian times to supply water to the industrial valleys and they too have become an attractive part of the landscape

The Park is certainly blessed with a remarkable variety of scenery, which includes shapely summits, sharp ridges, glacier-worn valleys, limestone gorges, spectacular waterfalls, fast flowing streams and pleasant rivers.

Through the passing centuries history has blended with scenery and the marks left by men from Prehistoric, Roman, Celtic, Norman and Industrial times can be seen throughout the area. It is also rich with Iron Age hill forts, mysterious standing stones, stone circles and round barrows. Norman Castles are numerous and they once guarded such locations as Abergavenny, Brecon, Crickhowell, Trecastle and Tretower, but the most dramatic of all is Carreg Cennen which is perched on top of a limestone crag. There are also many fascinating little churches founded by the wandering holy men of the sixth century and majestic ruins such as Llanthony Priory and Tretower Court.

Those who enjoy bird watching will delight in the mewing, circling flight of the buzzard, the dipper bobbing along river valleys and the plaintive call of the curlew. Skylarks may be heard singing loudly and seen flying with great energy while the occasional kite may be glimpsed in the west of the Park.

The best way to get to know any area intimately is by walking for many of the spectacular viewpoints and fascinating places that I have described can only be visited on foot. As for myself, I have walked, camped, caved and climbed in these hills for more than fifty years experiencing a wide range of weather conditions.

Descent of Cefn Cwm Llwch in the Brecon Beacons in challenging conditions

To know the Brecon Beacons National Park intimately you need to ascend the summits on numerous occasions and at varying times of the year. It is only then that you can fully appreciate their moods and ever-changing views. Also you need to not only follow the well established routes but also explore the lesser known ways as well.

In good winter conditions, I have enjoyed climbing the snow-filled gullies on the north-east face of Pen y Fan and on various occasion, navigated by compass across the mist shrouded wilderness of Fforest Fawr. I can recall countless walks in the 'Waterfall Country', photographing the beautiful cascades particularly amid the vivid colours of autumn. These places and areas all have their own special qualities and attractions to which I return time and time again.

My purpose in writing this guide book has been to provide helpful information to visitors to the area and to give local walkers further opportunities for enjoyment. By including items of historic interest, fascinating legends and up to date factual information, wherever possible, it has been my aim to encourage the reader to gain a deeper appreciation of the Brecon Beacons National Park.

Chris Barber
Llanfoist, 2009

TAKING TO THE HILLS

'I must not encumber myself with useless things.
Weight is my enemy, but at the same time I must not forget anything.'

Gaston Rébuffat

The mountains of the Brecon Beacons National Park provide ideal opportunities for hill walking but these grass and heather covered slopes and ridges can be deceptive to the unwary. Steep escarpments in particular should be treated with respect on misty or windy days.

Before going to the hills study the map and learn the general lie of the land. Work out 'escape routes' to be used in the event of bad weather. For example it will be noticed that the summits of the Brecon Beacons are fringed to the north, west and east with very steep slopes and fall away more gently to the south. The 'Roman Road' which traverses the Beacons from north to south provides an ideal 'escape route' because it is easily reached from several summits.

Most walkers today tend to be well clothed and equipped and the following reminders will be generally familiar to most readers, but they are included to give guidance to hill walkers of limited experience.

Mountain Safety Guidelines

1. Check weather forecasts and seek local advice. The Local Weathercall Number is 01898 500414). Information can also be obtained from the Brecon Beacons National Park Visitor Centre at Libanus. (Tel: 01874 623366).

2. Do not walk alone unless you are confident of your experience and ability.

3. Good leadership for novices venturing on the hills is essential. If forced to split up someone should take charge of each group.

4. Plan walks with a generous time allowance. Be prepared to turn back or change your route if the weather deteriorates. A useful way to plan your route is to use Naismith's rule:-
'Allow one hour for every 5km (3 miles)
and add 30 minutes for every 300m (1000 feet) of ascent'.

Time must also be added for refreshment and rest stops or difficult weather conditions. By using this formula one can estimate the time required for any walk quite accurately. But for safety, always allow more time than is really necessary.

---

5. If you intend to lead a party around an unfamiliar walk, particularly where the approach or finish crosses farmland, it is a good idea to check the route beforehand so that you can be sure of finding the right way. Your followers will be particularly impressed with the quality of your leadership if you appear to know the route so well that you hardly bother to use the map!

6. Suitable clothing and footwear should be worn. Even in summer carry a spare sweater and always take waterproofs for seemingly good weather can easily change. Remember that the temperature on the ridges and summits is certain to be considerably lower than in the valleys. During winter take additional items such as gloves, hat and extra sweater. In exceptional conditions when the summits are encrusted with ice or hard snow, an ice axe may also be advisable.

7. Always carry Ordnance Survey 1:25,000 or 1:50,000 maps and a compass and know how to use them.

8. Carry reserve food, torch, spare bulb / batteries, whistle and first aid kit, spare sweater, and emergency rations.

9. In the event of an accident, seek the nearest telephone. Dial 999 and state the nature of injuries and the location. The injured should be kept warm with all spare clothing, and if possible should not be left alone.

10. Make sure that you are familiar with the Mountain Distress Signal. Six long whistle blasts, torch flashes or shouts in quick succession and repeated at one minute intervals. To indicate that help is on the way: three long signals per minute should be given. These internationally recognised signals should be used only in cases of emergency.

Most people who venture into the hills these days are familiar with the Country Code but the abbreviated version which originated in America is always worth quoting:-

> 'Take nothing but photographs; kill nothing but time.
> Leave nothing behind but your footprints and goodwill.'

Maps to use with this guidebook

This guide is based on the Ordnance Survey Outdoor Leisure Series maps: sheets 12 and 13. Scale:1:25000 (4cm to 1 km or 2.5 inches to 1 mile). The simple sketch maps in this book are for basic guidance only, so the relevant OS map should always be carried and used in conjunction with the written descriptions of routes.

To convert metres to feet:-
(a) The rough and ready method:
    Divide by 3 and the result for a peak of 2,500 feet will be about 37 feet too much.

(b) The accurate way:
    Multiply the height in metres by 3.2808992.

To convert kilometres to miles:-
(a) The rough and ready method:
    Divide by 8, multiply by 5; the result will be about 50 feet too much in every mile.

(b) The accurate way:
    Divide by 1.609.

OPEN ACCESS IN THE BRECON BEACONS NATIONAL PARK

It is your right under the Countryside and Rights of Way (CROW) Act, to roam freely across mapped 'access land' and common land without having to stay on footpaths. Please remember however that much of the land is privately owned and is still used for grazing and water catchment. You must comply with any restrictions that are displayed at car parks and access points.

Detailed information is included on Ordnance Survey Explorer maps, shaded in yellow. In addition, information boards are located at key points in the National Park

'Maps are always a treasured possession of the mountaineer. They are the charts by which he steers his course, they enable him to plan his journeys beforehand, guide him in carrying out those plans, and above all, perhaps, they serve to recall his memories of great days spent amongst the hills. Maps are essential to a full enjoyment of his sport and under some conditions may be essential to his safety.'

G.A. Lister 1924

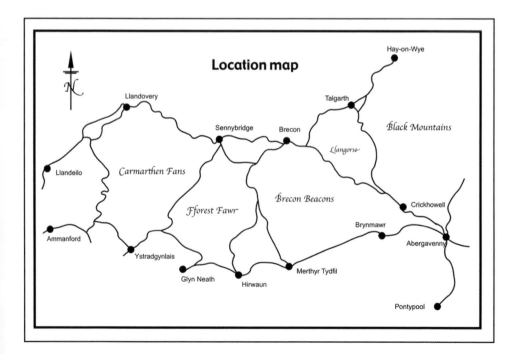

THE BLACK MOUNTAINS

'The Black Mountains of the Welsh - English Border are a singularly unspoilt group of long and lofty ridges separated by valleys of diversified charm, descending steeply towards the Wye on the northern side, and on the southern side less abruptly towards the Usk.'

P. Thoresby Jones

When travelling towards Gwent (or Monmouthshire as it is now known) from the Hereford direction one may pick out on the skyline a long black ridge. For many visitors to the area, this is their first sight of these mountains and the reason for their descriptive name is self-evident. From a distance, except when the sun is shining strongly on the nearest ridge, they really do look black. On a dull day in particular they appear as a large dark-hued wedge silhouetted against the grey of the sky. Some say it was the Saxons who provided the name for they always saw the mountains from the eastern side of the Wye.

Seen closer the colours may vary from green in summer sunlight to purple in late summer and russet when the bracken is dying in late Autumn to brilliant white in Winter after the snows have fallen.

The whole mountain mass is composed of Old Red Sandstone, apart from one single summit which displays a white crest of limestone and is appropriately named Pen-cerrig-calch 'Head of the White Crag.'

A.G. Bradley described the ridges and valleys of the Black Mountains as 'eighty square miles of complete, uncompromising solitude'. This may well have been so in his day, but the 'Blacks' are now much more popular with walkers and pony trekkers, so that particularly in summer, it is rare when one can roam across these summits without meeting other walkers or catch sight of a line of riders moving Red Indian fashion across the skyline.

The four main ridges average 17.6 km (11 miles) in length and 600m (2,000 ft) in height. Waun Fach at 811m (2,660 ft) is is the highest summit but Pen y Gadair Fawr 800m (2,624 ft) is a more attractive peak and even looks higher. At the north end of the ridges is a plateau terminating in an escarpment which overlooks the Wye Valley.

It is easy to remember the layout of the Black Mountains if you relate them to your right hand placed flat on a table with the fingers spread apart. Your thumb is Crib y Garth or 'Cat's Back'. Your first finger is Hatterrall, your second finger is Ffawyddog, with Bal Mawr at the knuckle. Your third finger is the Gader ridge. Your little finger is Allt Mawr, and its nail is Crug Hywel, giving its name to Crickhowell below it. On the back of your hand are Twyn y Llech and Twmpa, Rhos Dirion and Waun Fach. This is undoubtedly the best way to visualise the five ridges and four valleys of this compact and unique range.

Llanthony Priory in the Vale of Ewyas

ROUTE 1
The Llanthony Circuit

17 km (10.5 miles) and 670m (2197 feet) of ascent

'The Vale of Ewyas, more commonly known perhaps as the Llanthony Valley, is among the gems in Wales.'

A.G. Bradley 1911.

START: Public car park at Llanthony Priory (GR 289278 OL13)

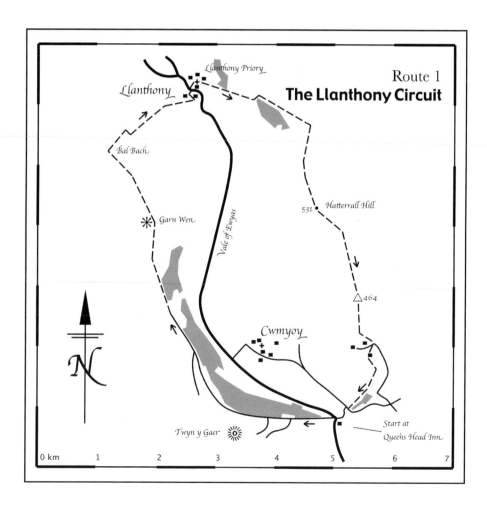

ROUTE DIRECTIONS

1) Go through a gate to the left of Abbey Farm and walk around the back of the priory, beside a stone wall to go through a gate. Then follow the left hand field boundary to reach a gatenear the top right corner.

(2) Follow a track through Wirrall Wood to reach a wooden gate and then walk straight up the next field. keeping the fence on your right to another gate. Turn right to follow a well worn track (signposted Cwmyoy) which in due course gently ascends the hillside, providing fine views into the valley. This ancient route, known as the Rhiw Cwrw or 'beer track' was once used by the monks transporting casks of beer between Llanthony and Longtown on the other side of the ridge.

(3) On reaching the crest of the ridge, turn right to follow a section of the Offa's Dyke National Trail, (268km or 168 miles) in length. It connects Chepstow near the Severn withPrestatyn on the North Wales coast. The view to the west extends to the Shropshire Long Mynd, Clee Hills, Malvern Hills, Graig Syffrydin and the Forest of Dean. Pass a trig' point on the left and make your way down towards Pentwyn Iron Age hill fort.

(4) Descend to join a stone wall and a cart track leading to a farm on the right. Cross a stone stile set into the wall on the right (easily missed). Head down through a field towards a barn. Walk past a ruined farmhouse, through a gate and then almost immediately go through the left hand of two gates. Make your way down through the next field, bearing slightly right. On reaching a stile, cross the next field to another stile and then walk straight down through the next field to reach a stile beside a gate. Head down the centre of the next field to reach a stile beside a gate in the bottom left hand corner of the field. Walk down through the next field keeping a fence on the left to reach a stile in the bottom left hand corner. Descend some steps and emerge onto a road with care. Turn left and shortly left again and make your way via a stone bridge and then uphill to the Queens Head Inn.

(5) Just north of the inn, turn left and ascend a road leading steeply up towards the Gaer hill fort which is a fine example of a fortified camp of the Iron Age period. It is oval in shape and encloses an area of just under 5 acres. After a seemingly endless ascent, the road becomes a cart track, which brings you to a gate and the open hillside. Here one may make a detour to inspect the earthworks of the hill fort or keep straight on along the main track. On the right are views into the Llanthony Valley, which is also known as the Vale of Ewyas. Across the valley can be seen the Darren, a crumbling Old Red Sandstone cliff.

Dialgarreg - 'the Stone of Revenge'

Garn Wen a fine circular cairn built by a local craftsman

19

In due course one encounters a small stone about 1 metre high, set into the ground beside the track. It is known as Dialgarreg and also 'the Stone of Revenge', for it marks the spot where in 1135 Richard de Clare, a Norman knight was ambushed and murdered by a band of Welshmen led by Morgan ap Owen.

(6) Continue along the crest of the ridge to reach the prominent cairn of Garn Wen (White Stones). This very fine circular cairn has obviously been built with tender care and a craftman's skill. After about a mile another cairn is reached, below the hump of Bal-Mawr (607m). Turn right and descend towards Llanthony.

(7) Take a track to the right, leading down into Cwm-bwchel and follow a stony shelf down the side of the valley. Soon, Llanthony Priory will be seen nestling in the valley below and this is a good path from which to admire its magnificent setting

View of Llanthony Priory from Cwm-bwchel

'In this deep Vale of Ewyas about an arrow shot broad and encircled on all sides by lofty mountains is a situation truly calculated for religion and more adapted to canonical discipline than all the other monasteries of the British Isles.'

Giraldus Cambrensis 1188

(8) **On reaching a stile, follow waymarks down to another stile. Go over the stile and continue between two fences to reach two stiles side by side. The one on the left is on the route of a permitted path which avoids problems of unpleasant farmyard mud. Follow the path through a field to reach a stile beside a gate. Then go right over another stile. Cross a long footbridge spanning a stream and keep straight on following waymarks which lead you down through a field.**

(9) **Negotiate two stiles in quick succession (with a dingle in between) and go left, following the edge of a field to reach a stile beside a gate. Now cross a metal footbridge spanning the Afon Honddu and follow a track into the peaceful hamlet of Llanthony. Walk up the lane directly opposite to reach Llanthony Priory.**

The name, Llanthony is a corruption of Llan-Honddu (the church on the Honddu) or, more fully, Llan Dewi Nant Honddu (the Church of St David on the river Honddu). According to tradition, the first simple church was erected here by St David (Dewi) in the 6th century when he spent some years meditating in this remote place.

Llanthony Priory was founded in about 1107 by William de Lacy who was a brother of the Lord of Ewyas. Roger, Bishop of Salisbury, was responsible for much of the design and the west front is said to resemble portions of Salisbury Cathedral. The south tower and prior's house now serves as a hotel.

The Abbot's Lodgings, now known as the 'Abbey Hotel'

Llanthony Priory in the Vale of Ewyas

The Augustinian monks, apparently found the Welsh locals too unfriendly and the weather even worse. One monk even recorded in his journal that he had 'no mind to sing to the wolves'. In 1136 the monks retreated to Gloucester where they founded a new priory which they also called Llanthony. Only a handful of monks were left in this Black Mountain valley and Llanthony gradually became used as a place of banishment where offending brothers were sent to serve penance.

The poet, Walter Savage Landor, bought the estate in 1808 with grandiose ideas of reforming the Priory to its former glory, but he quarrelled with his tenants and neighbours who obviously did not share his dreams. In 1813 he left the valley for good, having squandered £70,000 on the estate. He wrote: 'I shall never cease to wish that Julius Caesar had utterly exterminated the whole race of Britons. I am convinced that they are as irreclaimable as gypsies or Malays,' He died in Florence in his 90th year in 1864.

'About a mile above Llanthony we descried the Abbey ruins, the dim grey pile of building in the vale below standing by the little riverside among its brilliant green meadow.'

Rev Francis Kilvert 1870

ROUTE 2
Capel -y-ffin Northern Circuit

19.5 km (12.11 miles) and 613 m (2010 feet) of ascent

'Daren Lwyd, a flawless grass dome that closes in the valley.'

H.J. Massingham, 1950

START: Capel-y-ffin hamlet. Park on grass verge GR 255313 (OL13)

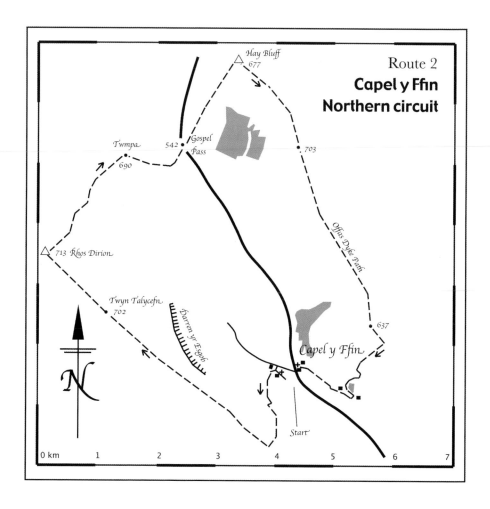

The little white washed church surrounded by ancient yew trees is well worth a quick visit before starting this walk. Its name translates as 'Chapel on the boundary' and it stands close to the old counties of Breconshire and Monmouthshire. It is little larger than a cottage and has a slatted wooden bell-turret astride the roof. When the Reverend Francis Kilvert came here in 1870 he later referred to it in his diary as being 'short stout and boxy, with its little bell-turrett, the whole building reminding me of an owl.'

ROUTE DIRECTIONS

(1) **Just south of the church go up a lane leading to the Nant y Bwch Valley. After about a quarter of a mile turn left up a lane leading to Capel-y-ffin Monastery** which is now a private home. This was founded by Father Ignatius in 1870. He was a man with a great gift of oratory and his aim was to revive the Benedictine monastic life in the Church of England. However, his dream came to an end when he died in 1908 and the three monks who were left soon departed to join the Benedictine Abbey on Caldey Island near Tenby.

On the side of the road leading to the monastery is a wooden calvary erected in memory of Father Ignatius. **Turn right to pass the Grange Trekking Centre. A stony path, much eroded by pony trekking is then followed to reach more level ground above. Cross a stream and head towards the escarpment of Tarren yr Esgob. Follow a well defined track which ascends the steep hillside in a series of zig zags to reach a cairn.**

(2) **Continue up to the crest of the ridge and then head north-west to reach Twyn Tal-y-cefn (702m). From there continue to Rhos Dirion trig' point (713m) and the edge of the north escarpment** where impressive views across the Wye Valley may be obtained. In the distance to the west can be seen the Carmarthen Fans while in the near distance stand the Brecon Beacons. To the north may be seen the hills of Radnor Forest.

(3) **Turn right along the edge of the escarpment and descend to the head of the Nant bwch Valley. (One may shorten the route now by following a pleasant track down the valley to Capel-y-ffin).**

(4) **A short ascent now leads to a cairn on the summit of Twmpa (690 m) and from there a well worn track leads you down to the mountain road at a point known as the Gospel Pass. Cross the road and follow the path up to the summit Hay Bluff.** This is another fine vantage point.

St Mary's Church, Capel-y-ffin

Capel-y-ffin Monastery was founded by Father Ignatius in 1870

(5) Now head south east and continue down the ridge following the Offa's Dyke National Trail for about 3 miles. to reach a crossing of tracks. Turn right and head down towards the Llanthony Valley. After passing a prominent stone go left at a T junction and follow the path down towards the steep cwm on the left. The track bends to the right and on reaching another junction, follow the track to the left back towards the cwm. It then curves around to the right and descends to a fence.

(6) On reaching the fence, turn right. Go left over a stile and descend steeply. Cross another stile and on meeting a fence turn right. Cross a stream and head down to the left. A stile and steps lead down to a road.

(7) Go right through a gate and follow the road - through another gate - then continue along the road which soon becomes a wide track running between hedges.

(8) Pass through a gateway and cross a stream in a gully. Climb steeply up some stone steps and cross a stile. Head straight across a field - go over a stile - cross the next field - cross a stile - cross the next field and walk on to reach a gate. Now continue along a broad track looking down on the Honddu. Go past an old stone cottage and then through a gate. Follow the stony path down into the valley. Pass through another gate and past a chapel on the right. Cross a bridge and climb over a stone stile to enter the churchyard and follow a path around the edge of the churchyard wall. Go through a gate and onto the road at Capel-y-ffin.

'How glad everything is looking! Now the noisy Honddu shines like silver in the sun and joins its music to the sheep's bleat, the oxen's low, the bird's song, the bee's hum, the breeze's breath.'

Father Ignatius 1870

ROUTE 3
Capel -y-ffin Southern Circuit

15.25 km (9.4 miles) and 770 m (2525 feet) of ascent

'Like a rush of molten silver seemed the Honddu in the moon-glow; solemn were the dark shades which the Abbey-buildings cast, broad and long, upon the Abbot's meadow, the ineffable beauty of the mountains brooding over all.'

Father Ignatius

START: Capel- y- ffin hamlet. Park on the grass verge GR 255313 (OL13)

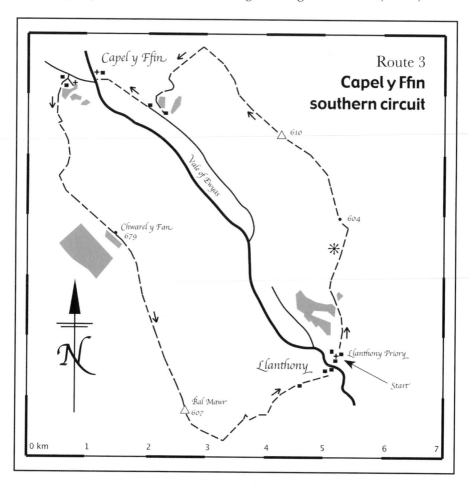

ROUTE DIRECTIONS

(1) Just south of the church follow a lane leading to the the Nant Bwch Valley. After about a quarter of a mile turn left up a lane leading to the Monastery. Shortly, turn right to pass the Grange Trekking Centre and follow a stony path, much eroded by pony trekking, to reach level ground above. Cross a stream and head towards the escarpment of Tarren yr Esgob. Follow a well defined track which ascends the hillside in a series of zig zags to reach a cairn.

(2) Continue up to the crest of the ridge and then head south west to reach a large cairn on the summit of Chwarel y Fan (679 m), where the hollows formed by old quarries provide good shelter from the wind.

(3) Continue along the ridge to take in the summit of Bal Mawr (607 m) and then descend to the col at Bal-bach and follow a track towards Llanthony.

(4) Take a track on the right, leading down into Cwm-bwchel and follow a stony shelf down the side of the valley.

(5) On reaching a stile, follow waymarks down to another stile. From here the right of way has been diverted. Go over a stile and continue between two fences to reach two stiles side by side. The one on the left is the route of a permitted path which avoids problems caused by very unpleasant farmyard mud. Follow the path through a field to reach a stile beside a gate. Then go right over another stile. Cross a long footbridge spanning a stream and keep straight on following waymarks which lead you down through a field.

(6) Cross two stiles in quick succession and go left, following the edge of a field to reach a stile beside a gate. Now cross a metal footbridge spanning the Afon Honddu and follow a track into the sleepy hamlet of Llanthony. Walk up the lane directly opposite to reach the Priory.

(7) Go over a stile (beside a gate) near the farmhouse and follow the path around a wall to another stile. Join a wide track and follow it straight across the field to reach a stream. Cross a stile and walk uphill to a gateway. Continue through the next field passing large dead trees to reach a stile in the top left hand corner. Carry on steeply to a stile which gives access to the hillside above. This is a good spot to pause and admire the view of the Llanthony Valley.

The Vale of Ewyas from Loxidge Tump

(8) **Continue uphill towards some thorn bushes and then bear right towards a group of trees. Walk steeply upwards to reach a path, heading around above Cwm Siarpal. Strike up to the ridge above to join Offa's Dyke Path. Turn left and follow it northwards towards Hay Bluff.** This is the border of England and Wales and one can walk with one foot in Wales and the other in England. There is a complete contrast in views to the left and right

(9) **Pass the Ordnance Survey trig' point (610m) and 1.6km (1 mile) beyond it a crossing of tracks is reached which is shown on the map as 'pile of stones'. Turn left and follow a path down towards the Llanthony Valley. After passing a prominent stone go left at a T junction and follow the path down towards the steep cwm on the left. The track bends to the right and on reaching another junction follow the track to the left back towards the cwm. It then curves around to the right and descends to a fence.**

(10) **On reaching the fence, turn right. Go left over a stile and descend steeply. Go over another stile and on meeting a fence turn right. Cross a stream and head down to the left. A stile and steps lead down to a road.**

(11) **Go right through a gate and follow the road - through another gate - then continue along the road which soon becomes a wide track running between hedges. Pass through a gateway and cross a stream in a gully. Climb steeply up some stone steps and cross a stile. Head straight across a field - go over a stile - cross the next field - cross a stile - cross the next field and walk on to reach a gate. Now continue along a broad track looking down on the river Honddu. Go past an old stone cottage and then through a gate. Follow the stony path down into the valley. Go through another gate and past a chapel on the right. Cross a bridge and go over a stone stile to enter the churchyard and follow a path around the edge of the churchyard wall. Go through a gate and onto the road at Capel-y-ffin.**

'Looking south I could see every detail of the Vale of Ewyas, with the Skirrid rising finely at its lower extremity, and the Sugar Loaf looming more hazily on the right.'

A.G. Bradley 1911

ROUTE 4
Blaen-y-cwm Circuit

15.5 km (9.63 miles) and 440 m (1443 feet) of ascent

'The Black Mountains of the Welsh speaking Border are a singularly unspoilt group of long and lofty ridges, separated by valleys of diversified charm.'
P. Thoresby Jones 1938

START: Car Park at Blaen-y-cwm in the Grwyne Fawr Valley GR 252285 (OL13). Make sure that you observe the warning notice that this car park will be locked at a certain time in the early evening.

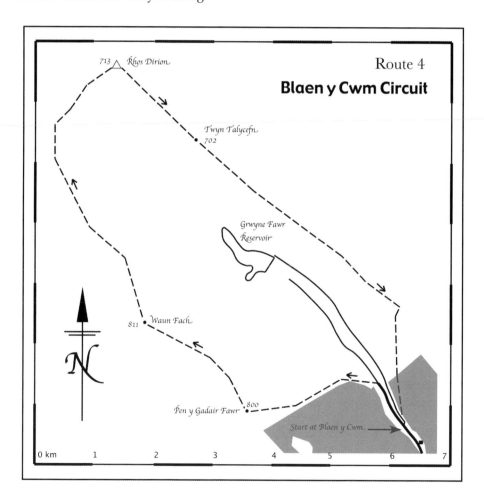

ROUTE DIRECTIONS

(1) **From the car park follow the road north for about 500 metres and go over a footbridge. Turn right along the river bank and walk on to shortly reach a stile. Cross the stream flowing down on the left and then ascend a track heading up the bank on the right of the stream. It becomes rather indistinct and leads up the open hillside providing a fairly gradual ascent of Pen y Gadair Fawr.** The summit is marked with a cairn, and this is undoubtedly one of the best viewpoints in the Black Mountains (800m).

(2) **Now follow a well worn track to Waun Fach across the peaty ridge to reach the summit plateau of Waun Fach (811m).** The summit is marked by the concrete base of the long vanished trig' point. **Continue along the path to Pen y Manllwyn to reach the north escarpment.** From here on a clear day there are fine views of the upper Wye Valley, the Begwyns and Radnor Forest.

Below is the lonely Grwyne Fawr Reservoir with its high dam bridging the narrow valley. At one time this was the highest reservoir in Britain and also the greatest in depth. The dam is built on a curve and the top level of water is 590m above sea level and it is 40 metres deep with a capacity of 376 million gallons. The dam is 327 metres long and 43 metres wide at the bottom and 6 metres wide at the top. Pipes were laid for a distance of 51 km (32 miles) to carry the water via Pont Esgob, around the east side of the Sugar Loaf to Abergavenny, under the River Usk, through Govilon, up to Waunavon and then by tunnel to Abertillery.

(3) For a quick return to the starting point, turn right to follow the track down to the Grwyne Fawr Reservoir and then on to meet the valley floor near the car park.

For a longer walk continue as follows:-

(4) Follow the edge of the escarpment to reach the trig' point on Rhos Dirion (713m). Now head in a south-easterly direction along the ridge to take in Twyn Talycefn (702m). Continue along the crest of the ridge almost as far as Chwarel y Fan (679m) and descend to the end of a forestry plantation. Follow a path down to join the reservoir track and turn left to head down to the Car Park at Blaen-y-cwm.

'Above my head two pairs of buzzards endowed empty space with life and form and grace and the merry growl of a raven hidden among the steep slopes gave it a voice.'

H.J. Massingham 1950

The Grwyne Fawr Reservoir

The workers' village built at Blaen y Cwm was known as 'Tin Town'

ROUTE 5
Llanbedr Horseshoe

27 km (16.75 miles) 972 m (3188 feet) of ascent

'The Penalltmawr ridge provides almost all that a walker and nature-lover can demand, including solitude and much wildlife.'

Norman G. Brett-James 1942

START: Llanbedr Village GR 239204 (OL13). Parking here can often be a problem due to limited space. It is sometimes better to park in a lay by near a road junction west of the village (SN 234203) and then walk back into the village.

ROUTE DIRECTIONS

(1) From the church follow a lane due east passing some old cottages. The tarmac surface soon becomes a rough track steeply descending to the river Grwyne. Cross a stone bridge and on the other side follow a path up a steep bank. Ignore a path to the right when half-way up the bank.

(2) At the top of the bank go over a stile and head straight up the next field with a fence on the left. Go over a stile, cross a lane, ascend some steps and cross the stile directly opposite. Walk straight across the next field to go over a stone slab stile in the fence on the right which is followed immediately by a wooden stile. Head straight up through the middle of the next field and make for a stile beside a gate just above the attractive house called Hen Bant. Then bear left to the top left hand corner to a stile by a fence. (Ignore the small stile lower down on the left). Turn left up a stony track ascending beside a moss covered stone wall and go through a gate. The track leads on with pleasant views into the valley and passes the remains of an old building on the right, to reach a gate.

(3) Beyond the gate the track curves around to the right and ascends the lower slopes of Blaen-yr-henbant providing fine views of Ysgyryd Fawr (Skirrid Fawr) and Mynydd Pen-y-fal (Sugar Loaf). Pass below the summit of Crug Mawr (550m), or detour to include it. Soon the crest of the ridge is reached where one can look down into the Grwyne Fawr valley. At Disgwylfa is a small cairn (540m).

(4) Continue along the crest of the ridge via Pen Gwllt-meirch and Pen-twyn-mawr (658m). From here the track continues to the hump of Pen-y-Gadair Fawr (Top of the Great Chair), where the summit is marked by a large pile of stones (800m). To my mind this is the finest viewpoint in the Black Mountains although it is surprisingly lower than the neighbouring and less interesting summit of Waun Fach.

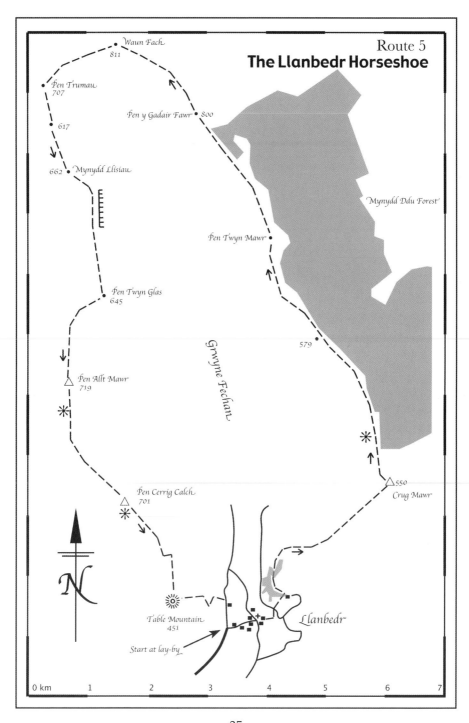

Route 5
The Llanbedr Horseshoe

Waun Fach
811

Pen Trumau
707

617

662 Mynydd Llisiau

Pen y Gadair Fawr 800

Mynydd Ddu Forest

Pen Twyn Mawr

Pen Twyn Glas
645

Gwyne Fechan

579

Pen Allt Mawr
719

550
Crug Mawr

Pen Cerrig Calch
701

Table Mountain
451

Start at lay-by

Llanbedr

N

0 km   1   2   3   4   5   6   7

View from summit of Crug Mawr, looking north

19th century boundary Stones on Pentwyn Glas

Summit of Pen Allt-mawr

The track leads down from Pen Cerrig-calch to Table Mountain (Crug Hywel)

(5) **Descend on the north side and continue over a usually boggy plateau to reach the summit of Waun Fach** which aptly translates as 'Small Bog' (811m). It is marked by the base of a trig' point which was removed many years ago making the summit very difficult to locate on a misty day.

(6) **Head west and descend Pen Trumau to reach a cairn. From here make a short ascent to Mynydd Llysiau (662m) and follow the ridge to reach Pentwyn Glas (645m)** which is marked by 19th century boundary stones. They bear the names of local landowners - (Mrs Macnamara 1811 and Sir J. Bailey Bart MP 1847) - whose estate boundaries met at this point. They are NOT gravestones as some people imagine!

(7) Pen Allt-mawr now looms in the distance. This is the steepest climb on the walk. **Ascend it directly or follow a diagonal track on the right to reach the summit trig' point** (719m) and a large stone windbreak. This is an excellent viewpoint.

(8) **Continue, passing Pen Gloch-y-pibwr on your right (or make a detour to take it in) and proceed to the final peak on the ridge, Pen Cerrig-calch (701m).** You will pass curiously eroded limestone outcrops, providing an interesting geological feature, for this is the only Carboniferous limestone in the Black Mountains, and was once part of the Llangattock escarpment, before the Usk Valley was formed.

(9) **From the trig' point continue in a south-easterly direction to follow a track leading down to Crug Hywel** appropriately known as Table Mountain (451m). The town of Crickhowell takes its name from this fort which is associated with Hywel ap Rhys of Morgannwg and not Hywel Dda as is frequently supposed. It is a fort of simple design with only one rampart and dates back to the Iron Age (450 BC to 43 AD). There are about 3000 hill forts in Britain and 200 of these are located in Wales. The village of Llanbedr will now be seen directly below.

(10) **Descend towards Llanbedr and make for a stile beside a gate in the corner of a stone wall**. It is directly above two barns which have been converted into an outdoor activity centre called Perth-y-pia. **Continue your descent through the next field to reach a stile near the centre and then follow the steep concrete drive down to a road. Turn right along the road and after passing Ty mawr Farm, take the next turning on the left which leads back to Llanbedr.**

'Here the confirmed ridge-walker can indulge to the full his strange predilection: he can ridge-walk all day every day for a week and still find unfamiliar spurs to traverse.'

P. Thoresby Jones 1938

ROUTE 6
Pengenffordd Circuit

'The John Bradley Memorial Route'

11 km (6.8 miles) and 575 (1886 metres) of ascent

'Y Grib, whose sharply terraced or notched backbone leads out east to Pen y Manllwyn, the nasal front of the Gader Ridge walling the Grwyne Fawr headwaters.'

H.J. Massingham, 1950

START: A small car park GR 176303 (OL13) on the side of a lane which runs in a north-easterly direction from the highest point of the Crickhowell to Talgarth road (A479). Alternatively, park at the Castle Inn, beside the A479 (small fee to be paid).

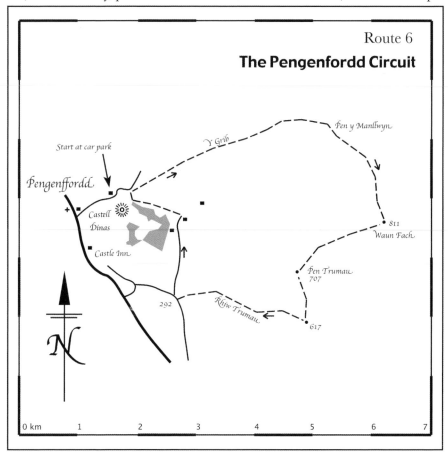

I have dedicated this walk to my old friend John Bradley whose untimely death from a heart attack at the age of 51 occurred on this route in February 1986. John was the first Brecon Beacons National Park Officer to be appointed, a post he held for 12 years. He had previously been employed by Monmouthshire County Council for ten years with a special responsibility for the management of the National Park in that area. John was one of the most experienced and respected professionals working in landscape conservation and countryside recreation at that time. He was also an enthusiastic mountaineer with an extensive knowledge of British mountains and the Alps. John and I shared many roped ascents and some enjoyable walks and he is sadly missed by all who had the privilege of knowing him.

ROUTE DIRECTIONS

(1) Follow the lane up to a gate and from there make for the end of the ridge of Y Grib. Take the direct way up the centre of the ridge. After the initial steep ascent it becomes more gradual and then rises in a series of humps, which have resulted in it being affectionately known as the 'Dragon's Back'. To the right one looks down into the lovely Rhiangoll Valley and across the Pen Allt-mawr ridge.

(2) After the second hump on the ridge, a short descent leads to a shoulder where various tracks meet to provide alternative routes to this point, from the valleys on either side. From here the track is clearly defined and follows the left hand side of the ridge. Some walkers prefer to follow the crest of the ridge, but the lower track provides a more direct route to the next dip in the ridge.

(3) Crossing the next hump, the track passes over rocks which provide an exhilarating situation and good views. Soon a small cairn is reached and the ridge becomes flatter and broader. On reaching a junction, turn right and head for Pen y Manllwyn.

Looking to the north one can appreciate the solitude of the terminal plateau of the Black Mountains. On the skyline to the east is the Hatterrall ridge which forms part of the Offa's Dyke Long Distance footpath.

(4) Soon you will reach the summit of Pen y Manllwyn and from there continue along an often boggy track to reach the summit of Waun Fach (811m), which in mist can be hard to locate. The trig' point disappeared many years ago and the concrete base is surrounded by a pool. The meaning of Waun Fach is 'Little Bog' and it can certainly live up to its name.

Looking down Y Grib, popularly known as the 'Dragon's Back'

View from Bwlch Trumau

(5) **From the west side of the plateau a path descends to Pen Trumau. On reaching the blunt end of this ridge go down to the col and then follow a track to the right. This is the Rhiw Trumau and it offers an easy descent to a tree-lined sunken lane leading down to a tarmac road. Turn right and you have a choice of finishes. If you wish to visit the Castle Inn for well earned refreshment then take the next turning on the left. Otherwise, ignore this turning and follow the road to pass a farm and then go up a track on the left. It is deeply rutted and leads up via two gates to pass through a col. A stile on the left** gives access to the remains of Castell Dinas, a Norman Castle built within the ramparts of an Iron Age Hill Fort. There is very little stonework to be seen, but the short detour is well worth it, if only for the view. At an altitude of 450m (1,476) feet, Castell Dinas can claim to be the highest castle in England and Wales.

(6) **Otherwise continue to reach a gate on the left and rejoin your outward route which leads down to the car park in the lane.**

Castell Dinas is the highest Norman castle in England and Wales

ROUTE 7
Olchon Valley Circuit

15.5 km (9.6 miles) and 420 m (1377 feet) of ascent

'The deep valley of the Olchon swells the sparkling waters of the Monnow, and the Black Mountains throw out the long hog's back of Crib y Garth and Black Hill to hem the valley in.'

H. J. Massingham

START: Car Park/Picnic site GR 288328 (OL13) at Black Hill, off the mountain road beyond Longtown and Llanveynoe.

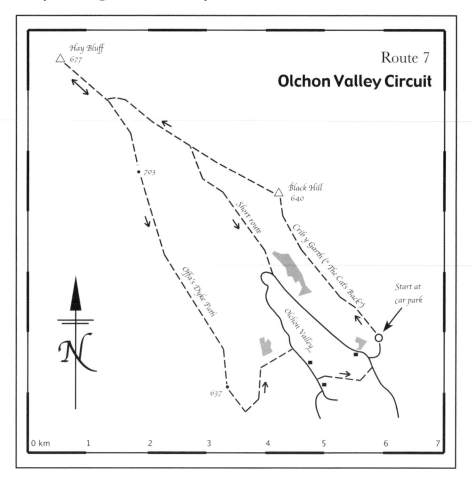

ROUTE DIRECTIONS

(1) **Cross the stile at the north end of the car park and head up the slope above. It is steep at first but before long the gradient becomes much easier**. To your left is the Hatterrall ridge carrying Offa's Dyke Path, and to the right is the more open patchwork-quilt view of Herefordshire. To the south lies the Longtown Valley with Graig Syfryddin to be seen in the distance.

(2) **The ridge which is popularly known as the Cat's Back becomes a series of rocky steps and a cairn is reached near some old quarries which provide useful shelter for a coffee stop. From here the ridge narrows for a few hundred yards and then broadens into Black Hill, the summit being marked by a trig' point (640m).**

(3) **Follow a well worn path north-west towards Hay Bluff. Where the track crosses the head of the Olchon Valley, the walk may be shortened by following a track down the valley, to join a road leading back to the start.**

(4) **The main route continues along the eastern side of the escarpment and curves around to join up with Offa's Dyke Path. From here it is a short distance to Hay Bluff which is marked by a trig' point (677m).**

(5) **Return now along Offa's Dyke Path. A short ascent leads to the high point of 703m, and then a long plod following a well worn path, brings you to a boundary stone set upright by the side of the track. Continue for a quarter of a mile to reach a cairn at GR 270319. Follow a narrow track to the left and descend the eastern side of the ridge on an ancient path which zig zags down the steep slope. On reaching a gate and a road, turn right.**

(6) **Follow the road past Olchon Court and about 100 metres beyond Beili-bach go over a stile to follow a diverted right of way. The path leads down beside a fence and a stream to reach a footbridge. Continue, bearing slightly right. Now follow the right hand side of the next field. The path now goes right to cross a stream just above a farmhouse and then joins a rutted gravel track which leads up to a gate. Turn left along the road and take the next turning on the right to return to your starting point.**

'The high bank of Hatterrall ridge is broad and soft; for many miles a rank growth of whinberry bushes densely matted with heather and bog grasses hold you knee high and sometimes much more.'

A.G. Bradley 1911

Crib y Garth - the 'Cat's Back'

On the narrow rocky ridge of Crib y Garth

ROUTE 8
Macnamara's Road

21.1km (13.2 miles) and 699m (2,236 feet) of ascent

START: Car Park at the Castle Inn, Pengenffordd GR174297 (OL13). Small fee to be paid at the pub.

ROUTE DIRECTIONS

(1) **Descend some steps at the left end of the car park and turn right along a lane which is followed to a small ford. The lane then bends sharply to the right and passes a riding centre. After 50 yards turn left to follow a lane between fences and continue through a series of gates. A steady ascent brings you to a cairn on the saddle between Pen Trumau and Mynydd Lysiau.**

2) **From the col descend a stony track leading down into the head of the Grwyne Fechan Valley to reach a sharp right-hand bend at the top of a well engineered broad green path** which is reputed to have been constructed by John Macnamara, a wealthy landowner.

The Rhiw Trumau leads down into the Grwyne Fechan valley

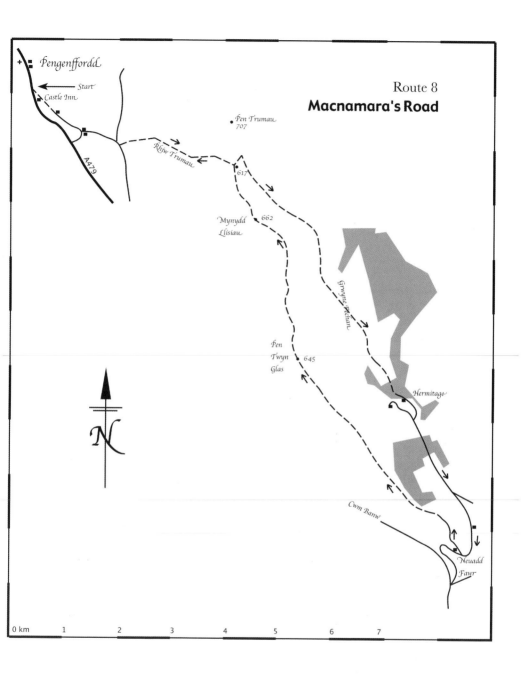

Pengenffordd

Start

Castle Inn

A479

Route 8
Macnamara's Road

Pen Trumau
707

Rhiw Trumau

617

Mynydd
Llisiau

662

Grwyne Fechan

Pen
Twyn
Glas

645

Hermitage

Cwm Banw

Neuadd
Fawr

N

| 0 km | 1 | 2 | 3 | 4 | 5 | 6 | 7 |

Tal-y-maes Bridge

Ruins of the Hermitage in Grwyne Fechan Valley

Old photograph of the Hermitage

(3) **Cross the bridge and follow the track, climbing the hillside and then passing through fields to descend steeply through a wood to reach the Hermitage. Follow the tarmac road to reach a small parking area in an old quarry. (GR234228).**

(4) **Go over a stile to the left of the parking area and bear right to follow a permissive path uphill, waymarked with posts. At the top of the field go through a gateway and turn left to follow a track which is signed 'To the Mountain'. In due course go through a gate and stay on the main track leading up the ridge with a wall on the left. After passing a plantation cross a stile and a large cairn will be reached on the crest of the ridge. The broad path leads on past old quarry workings and provides good views.**

(5) **On reaching Pen Twyn Glas (646m) keep straight on passing some boundary stones and then on along a broad path to the summit of Mynydd Llysiau (663m), which is a fine viewpoint. From there it is a short descent to Bwlch Trumau where the outward route is joined. Follow this back to the start.**

' The Grwyne Fechan is one of the least frequented and most beautiful valleys of the Black Mountains. In the early nineteenth century, nightingales resorted to its woods in great numbers according to Theophilus Jones.'

Dr. Margaret Davies 1967

ROUTE 9
Partrishow and Cwmyoy Churches
9.3km (5.8 miles) and 417m (.1,333 feet) of ascent

START: Park near a telephone box at the entrance to the Grwyne Fawr Valley at Five Lanes Junction, Fforest Coalpit GR284211 (OL13).

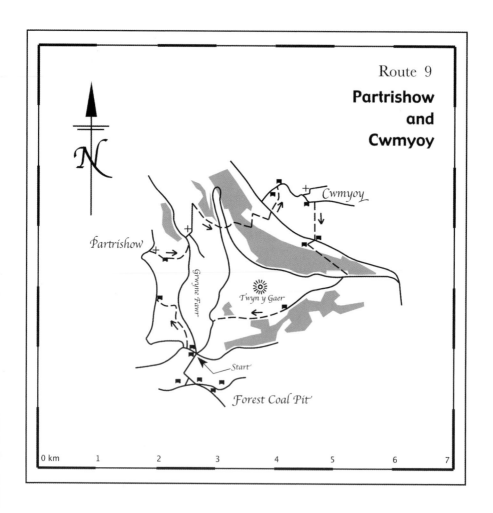

ROUTE DESCRIPTION

(1) **Make your way along the road to the left past the stone cottage to cross Pont Esgob (Bishop's Bridge) which spans the river Grwyne**. It was originally a packhorse bridge, but has been rebuilt in more recent years. The name recalls the time in 1188, when Archbishop Baldwin came to Wales, with Giraldus Cambrensis on a preaching tour, recruiting warriors for the Third Crusade.

(2) **At the next road junction go over a stile on the right and follow a path up through a field to reach a stile. Then bear right around some trees and continue through the next field. The path climbs gently through the next field and passes to the right of a ruined building and leads to a stile beside a gate. Go immediately left to ascend a fairly steep field to reach a stile. Then walk to the top right hand corner of the next field to cross a stone slab stile next to a cottage. Turn right along the quiet lane which leads you into Cwm Mair and shortly Partrishow Church will be seen perched on a shelf on the other side of the narrow valley.**

At a sharp bend where the Nant Mair brook tumbles beneath the road, some steps on the right lead down to a holy well which was once used by the hermit St Issui who settled here long ago and used its waters to baptise those who came here to accept the Christian faith. His kindness however, brought about his death, for one man who he had given shelter and sustenance murdered him. The well and his hermitage became a place of pilgrimage, and those who were sick found the water had curative powers. A wealthy 11th century traveller drank of the water and was cured of leprosy. He is reputed to have left a hatful of gold to build a church in gratitude for his recovery. The church was dedicated in honour of St Issui.

On the roadside above the well is a pilgrim stone incised with a Crusader's cross which was previously situated in the bank higher up the road. It is said to have marked the spot where Archbishop Baldwin once stood and preached to the local people.

(3) **Walk steeply uphill to shortly reach the lychgate of Partrishow Church.** Inside this neat construction is an inscription commemorating Richard Baker-Gabb, an Abergavenny man who did much to preserve the ancient church of Partrishow when it was disused and falling into ruin.

Situated at about 1,000ft above sea level, the oldest part of this remote little church dates back to 1060 and the chancel and western chapel were added in the 13th century. St Issui was the patron saint of this parish in the 11th century and Bishop Herewald of Llandaff, dedicated the church to him and named it Merthyr Yssui. As the centuries passed the name changed to Patricio and then Partrishow.

St Issui's Well

Partrishow Church

The western end of the church is separate to the nave and chancel and has been described as an Eglwys-y-bedd (church of the grave). It is possible that St Issui is buried beneath the altar of this separate chapel which is the earliest part of the church.

Inside the church is a beautiful 15th century carved screen carved in Irish oak, which has been left in its natural colour of silvery grey. It is one of the most beautiful examples of the woodcarvers' art to be found in Britain.

15th century Rood Screen, Partrishow Church

Also of interest are two stone altars, each bearing five consecration crosses; an ancient font which has a Latin inscription recording that it was made in the time of Genllin, an 11th century Prince of Powys and a 'dug-out' oak chest strengthened with iron bars and secured with three locks. In 1538 Thomas Cromwell ordered that every church should have such a chest (to be opened only when the posssessors of three keys were present), for the parish valuables.

There is a large royal coat of arms on the north wall and on the south wall texts include the Lord's Prayer and the Ten Commandments. On the west wall is a painting which some people find disturbing. It shows a skeleton representing the Reaper with a scythe, hour-glass and spade. This macabre figure is reputed to have been painted in human blood and it suggests to the departing visitor that judgement day is fast approaching.

(4) **Leave the eastern end of the churchyard through a small gate and go straight across a field to meet a track descending right past Ty'n-y-llwyn farmhouse.** The name means 'house in the grove' and it is a very attractive 15th century building, once owned by the Herbert family. It was converted into its present cross shape in 1649.

(5) **Immediately after the farmhouse turn left through a gate and cross a field. Then go over a stile and bear right down to another gate in the corner of a field. From there, go diagonally left to pass between two ruined buildings and follow the path descending into the valley to reach a stile. Cross a road and shortly, go over a bridge spanning the Grwyne Fawr to pass the Tabernacle Baptist Chapel (1837). Follow the road up to Ty Mawr Farm and then turn sharply right up a track gently ascending the hillside. On reaching a gate just below the crest of the ridge, keep straight on and make for a gate in the wall directly ahead. The path leads down the side of the valley, crossing a forestry track on the way, to reach the Llanthony road.**

(6) **Cross the road with care and go over a stile directly opposite and head for the bottom left hand corner of the field, where a stile brings you on to a road. Turn right, to cross the fiver Honddu on a bridge and follow the road uphill, to reach a point just below Cwmyoy Church. Turn up a track on the left which leads up to a metal kissing gate giving access to the churchyard.**

St Martin's Church is about 700 years old and appears to be toppling over. The tower leans towards the hillside at a crazy angle and the chancel tilts towards the valley. This is undoubtedly the most crooked church in Britain and tower even leans more than the world famous Tower of Pisa. The chancel has its axis out of line with the nave, representing, it is believed, the deflected head of Christ on Calvary, and the nave walls bulge outwards.

(7) **Follow the flagstone path through the churchyard to reach a road. Turn right and follow the road downhill, looking out for an old cider press on the right. Continue, passing (or visiting) 'Downey Barn Gallery' to reach a stile and fingerpost on the right. Walk through a field, keeping a fence on your right to reach a footbridge spanning the river Honddu. Follow the path to the left and it shortly bends right to reach a gate and then leads through the next field to a stile beside a house.**

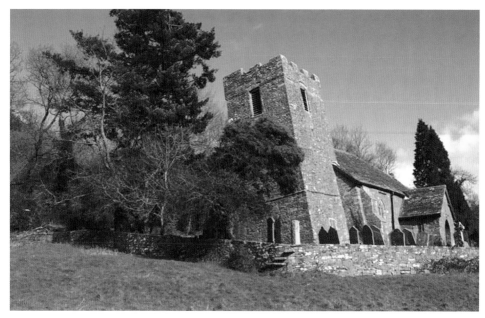

The leaning church at Cwmyoy

(8) **Cross the Llanthony road with care and go through a gate directly opposite to follow the drive leading to Coed Farm. On reaching the farm turn sharp left up a track leading diagonally up the hillside to reach a stile. This track rises at a reasonable angle and provides fine views into the valley. On reaching a forestry track go straight across and keep following the diagonal path. Also at the next junction keep on the diagonaly rising path to reach a stile and in due course it meets a road.**

(9) **Go right and immediately left to follow a broad and ancient track leading around the southern end of the Gader ridge.** It provides good views across Cwm Cerrig towards Skirrid Fawr, Bryn Arw and the Sugar Loaf. **In due course the track leads down past a small quarry to join a road. Turn left and follow it steeply down to your starting point at 'Five Lanes '.**

' The tower of Cwmyoy Church bends perilously towards the hillside, while the chancel threatens at any moment to disintegrate into the valley.'

Fred J. Hando 1958

ROUTE 10
Table Mountain from Crickhowell

5.7 km (3.6 miles) and 371m (1,187 feet) of ascent

'The small town of Crickhowell takes its name from Crug Hywel or Crucywell, a flat topped mountain, sometimes known as Table Mountain, capped by an Iron Age fort, north of the town.'

Edmund J. Mason 1975

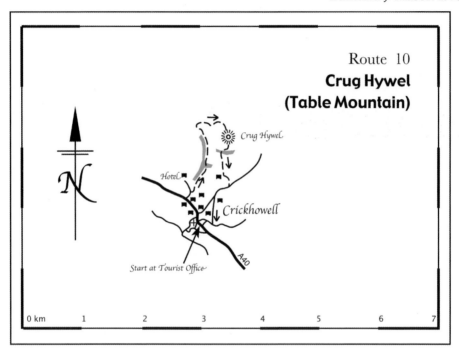

Route 10
**Crug Hywel
(Table Mountain)**

START: Car Park in Crickhowell, behind the Fire Station GR 218184(OL13)

ROUTE DIRECTIONS
(1) From the car park walk through the town towards Brecon, passing the Bear Hotel (voted the 'Best Pub in Britain' a few years ago). On reaching a school on the right, turn right up a metalled path and walk past the school to join a road, which bends around to the right. Shortly, turn left to follow a path between houses to reach a stile beside a gate. Follow the left edge of a field above a wooded valley containing the Cwmbeth Brook. In due course a stream is crossed and the path leads up to a stone walled sheep pen.

Crug Hywel, popularly known as Table Mountain gave its name to Crickhowell

(2) Follow the stone wall on the right and after ascending for a while, the path then contours to the right to reach the northern end of Crug Hywel, more popularly known as Table Mountain, because of its flat-topped appearance. However when you reach the summit you will find that it is not flat as the name suggests but slopes to the south. From here, there are excellent views across the Usk Valley towards Mynydd Llangattock. At 1,481 feet (451m) above sea level this is one of the highest hill forts in South Wales.

The town of Crickhowell takes its name from Crug Hywel (Hywel's Rocks) and this Iron Age fort has long been associated by guidebook writers, with Hywel Dda (Hywel the Good), a 10th century ruler of South Wales. However, my research has revealed that the Hywel who gave his name to the fort was in fact Hywel ap Rhys, the 9th century King of Glywysing. He made war on the lords of the land of Brycheiniog and established the boundary of his territory at 'Cerrig Hywel' with the erection of boundary stones.

(3) Descend at the southerly end of the fort and bear right to reach the corner of a stone wall. From here a waymarked path leads past a remote cottage and down through the fields to Ty-yn-y-Wlad farm. From there follow the road back to Crickhowell.

THE THREE PEAKS OF ABERGAVENNY

'To the north-west appears the magnificent Blorenge; on the north the elegant cone of the Sugar Loaf towers above the swell of the little Skyrrid, and to the east rises the abrupt ridge of the great Skyrrid.'

William Coxe 1801

The Three Peaks of Abergavenny (Blorenge, Sugar Loaf and Skirrid Fawr) have been made famous by an annual challenge walk which was originated by the author in 1963 and still attracts large numbers of entries. Distinctive in shape, these three hills offer varied and interesting routes to their summits and it is difficult to say which is the most satisfying peak for the views from all three are very extensive.

The Sugar Loaf or Mynydd Pen-y-fal to use its Welsh name rises to the north of the town and is separated from the Black Mountains by the valley of Grwyne Fawr. Its striking outlines are eye catching from every direction and it is so-named because it is said to resemble a heap of sugar when poured out of a bag. At 1,955 feet (596 metres) it just fails to reach the magic height of 2,000 feet, yet it always seems to be much higher for the approaches from all directions are quite long.

Skirrid Fawr or to use the true Welsh Ysgyryd Fawr is on the north-east side of Abergavenny and for various reasons it is also known locally as the 'Holy Mountain'. Ysgyryd is derived from Ysgur - to divide and this obviously stems from the strange shape of the hill for there is a dramatic notch on its western side where a large lump has slipped away from the summit.

There is a local tradition that this great cleft was gauged out by the bow of Noah's Ark during the Great Flood. It is of course a landslip caused by the inclination of the strata and the beds of intervening clay. An alternative explanation is that the slip occurred during the Crucifixion of Christ, when the hill was 'rent assunder by an earthquake and a bolt of lightning.'

The summit is encircled by the rampart of an Iron Age fort and just in front of the trig' point two upright stones and a depression in the ground mark the site of an ancient chapel dedicated to St Michael.

On the south side of Abergavenny is the bulky mass of the Blorenge which sometimes appears to frown on the town, but on a summer evening, when its northern slopes catch the evening light, it forms a serene and majestic backcloth. Blorenge is not a Welsh name and it has been suggested that the original Welsh was perhaps Blorens or even Blawreng meaning grey or blue ridge.

There is more to the Blorenge than the casual walker will at first appreciate, for it offers a wealth of interest ranging from prehistoric cairns to relics of the Industrial Revolution, which are important features in the Blaenavon Industrial Landscape World Heritage Site.

Mynydd Pen y Fal, popularly known as the Sugar Loaf

The Blorenge wearing its winter coat

Skirrid Fawr is also known as the Holy Mountain

ROUTE 11
Skirrid Fawr - The Holy Mountain

5.5 km (3.4 miles) and 296 m (970 feet) of ascent.

'On fair clear days we could see the pointed summit of the Holy Mountain by Abergavenny. It would shine I remember, a pure blue in the far sunshine: it was a mountain peak in a fairy tale.'

Arthur Machen

START: Park in a layby on the B4521 about three miles north-east of Abergavenny GR 329164 (OL13). Just a word of warning: do not leave valuables on view in your vehicle for this car park is sometimes prone to problems of theft.

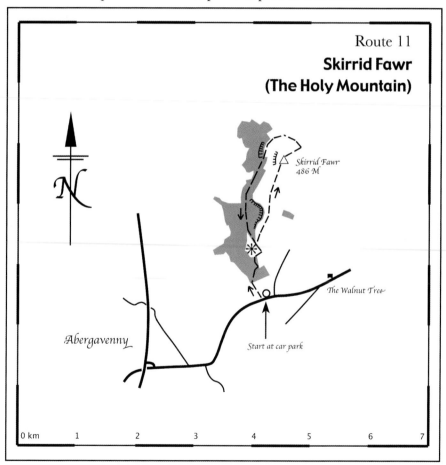

Route 11
**Skirrid Fawr
(The Holy Mountain)**

Skirrid Fawr
486 M

The Walnut Tree

Abergavenny

Start at car park

0 km   1   2   3   4   5   6   7

Skirrid Fawr rising above Abergavenny

View from summit of Skirrid Fawr towards the Sugar Loaf

ROUTE DIRECTIONS

(1) From the layby follow a sign-posted path between hedges to reach a stile on the edge of a wood. A well-trodden path then heads up through Caer Wood.

(2) On reaching the top of the wood, go over a stile and turn right to pass through a pleasant dingle. Soon the path brings you onto the open hillside and up to the start of a narrow ridge just over 1 km in length, which gently rises towards the summit.

The views are now open on both sides and on a clear day they can be very satisfying, with the distinctive the Sugar Loaf and the slumbering mass of the Black Mountains on the left contrasting with open rolling farmland on the east side of the ridge. In due course the trig' point will be seen in the distance marking the summit (486m). A short distance before the summit is a large chunk of rock with an assortment of initials and names carved on it.

The two stones were once part of the entrance to St Michael's Chapel

The summit is ringed by the oval fortification of an Iron Age fort that does not appear to have been completed. It is most noticeable on the north side of the summit, particularly as seen from a distance when sunlight picks out the line of the low rampart.

Just in front of the trig' point two upright stones and a depression in the ground mark the site of St. Michael's Chapel. The stones about 2 ft high with chamfered edges are all that remains of the doorway to the chape

(3) **One may complete a circular route by descending to the foot of the northern slope. Experienced walkers who are used to steep descents often use the direct route which goes down to the left. If you prefer a gentler route then either retrace your steps down the ridge or return along it for about 300 yards and take a path leading down diagonally on the left. This will also bring you to the foot of the northern slope and a track can then be followed around to the left to pass through the 'landslip valley'.** Years ago farmers used to dig large quantities of soil from this ravine and take it home by the sackful to sprinkle on their land to ensure a good harvest and keep the evil spirits away. The sacred soil was also sprinkled on coffins at funerals and some country folk even managed to convince themselves that it came from the Holy Land.

(4) **The path leads pleasantly through the valley.** A word of warning though, in summer it passes through high bracken which after a shower of rain will give your trousers a soaking.

On the hillside above you may notice a curious toadstool-shaped rock known as the 'Devil's Table'. We are told that his Satanic Majesty sat here having tea when Jack o' Kent leaped across the valley from the Sugar Loaf to leave his huge heel-print on the side of Skirrid Fawr.

(5) **Continue through the valley gently ascending through the woods and walk around the side of the hill to join a path which leads you around to the stile at the top of the stepped path on your outward route.**

'Waiting for the train, time is pleasantly spent in watching the changing effects of the last rays of sunset upon the rugged sides of the Skyrrid Mountain, which rises abruptly some two miles away.'

H. Thornhill Timmins 1892

The 'Devil's Table'

ROUTE 12
Skirrid Fawr - From the North

10.8km (6.75 miles) and 362m (1,158 feet) of ascent

'At some period, the night of the Crucifixion, say the locals, and call it in consequence "The Holy Mountain", a great landslip clave its summit in half, leaving one side precipitous, so that approaching it from two directions at any rate, it shows the outline of a complete though ragged peak, rising high above the wooded foreground.

A.G. Bradley 1913

Start: Park in the roadside atLlanfihangel Crucorney GR 325206 (OL13)

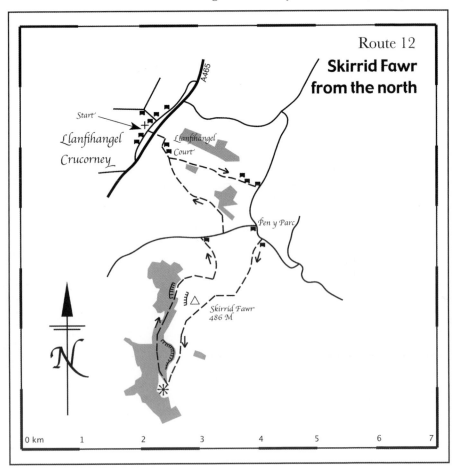

ROUTE DIRECTIONS

(1) **Go down a lane opposite the church and cross the A465 with extreme care, for the traffic moves very fast along this stretch of road. Continue down the lane on the other side, which is in fact the drive leading to Llanfihangel Court. On reaching the entrance gate follow the lane around to the right to shortly pass an impressive barn.**

(2) **When the lane divides, keep straight on, ignore a footpath sign to the right and continue along the lane beside a stone wall. Pass through a gate and after crossing a stream continue along a rutted track leading through the trees. Pass through a gate and the track starts to gently ascend to join a broader one. Keep straight on but shortly pause to look back for a distant view of Llanfihangel Court.**

This fine old house set in a wooded valley was built in Tudor times and it has been the home of many different families during the last 400 years. Both Queen Elizabeth I and Charles I are said to have stayed there and the coat of arms of the latter monarch, bearing the date 1594, is displayed in the drawing room.

Llanfihangel Court is a Tudor mansion set in a wooded valley

(3) **Shortly, turn right off the main track to cross a stream and go over a stile. Turn left and follow a fence to reach another stile.** There is a good view now looking back towards the Sugar Loaf. **Continue beside the fence and after about 100 yards go over a stile on the left, near a small derelict cottage. Continue up a sometimes muddy track to shortly enter a field on the left and head up to a stile beside a gate. On reaching a road, turn right and walk towards the prominent hump of Skirrid Fawr.**

The shapely profile of Skirrid Fawr

(4) **When a road junction is reached, keep straight on, and after about 200 yards, follow a track on the right leading up to a gate and a stile. Continue up the field beside a fenced gully which is an old hollow way.** Look directly left now to see the towers of White Castle perched on a hill-top.

The summit of Skirrid Fawr has been lost from view for a while, but it now appears gently rising above the top of the sloping field. Keep on beside the fence to go through a gate and cross an area of land known as the Arawllt. Continue through the next two fields and make for a stile in the top fence. Now head straight up for about 50 yards and then bear slightly left to pass a couple of trees.

(5) **Shortly you will join a broader track which diagonally ascends the steep northern side of Skirrid Fawr.** This is an ancient route which was established to provide an access to the summit chapel of St Michael Chapel and was probably used by the pilgrims who climbed this hillside several centuries ago. They came in large numbers on Good Friday and September 29th, which is St Michael's Day. **This track is not so steep as the direct northerly ascent route further around to the right and soon the angle relents slightly bringing you up to a point about 200 yards south of the summit (1595ft), which is reached by following the ridge to the right**.

The views on all sides can be very satisfying with the conical Sugar Loaf and the Black Mountains to the west contrasting with open rolling farmland on the east side of the ridge. Looking south one can see Abergavenny, the Blorenge and the Usk Valley.

Many walkers do not realise it but the summit of Skirrid Fawr is encircled by an Iron Age fort and just in front of the trig' point is an oblong depression in the ground which was once the site of a Roman Catholic chapel dedicated to St Michael. Only two upright stones now remain of the ancient building which measured 20 ft by 25 ft and was sited East - West. During the seventeenth century persecuted Catholics used to gather here in secret to hold mass eight or ten times a year. The chapel was demolished in 1680 by John Arnold of Llanfihangel Court.

6) **Having taken your fill of the view, either return by the same route or for a longer walk descend the spine ridge of the Skirrid for about one mile and then descend a path on the left, following the more popular route. On reaching a stile on the left where the path leads through the woods, ignore this turning and carry on beside a stone wall to make your way around the southern end of the hill. The path then continues through the trees and bracken along the lower slopes.**

In due course, ahead of you will be seen the famous Skirrid 'notch' through which the path passes, threading its way between boulders and slabs of rock. According to one local legend the notch was caused by Noah's ark as it glided over during the Great Flood. However legend also claims that this great cleft was created at the time of the Crucifixion of Christ when there was darkness over the land and Skirrid Fawr was struck by lightning causing it to shake violently and thus a ravine was formed.

Geologists of course tell us that the cleft is really a landslip which occurred as a result of the inclination of the strata and the beds of intervening clay. But a legendary explanation for a strange landscape feature is much more interesting!

Local farmers at one time certainly believed in the ancient tales for they used to fill sacks with soil taken from the great cleft and believing it to be sacred they sprinkled it on their fields to ensure a good harvest. The sacred soil was also sprinkled on coffins at funerals and some country folk even managed to convince themselves that it came from the Holy Land!

(7) **On the other side of this valley of rocks the path leads around to the base of the north face. Look out for two gates side by side, with a fence in between; go through the right hand one and head down beside a gully to reach a stile. Then bear left and follow the path down to reach a stile near a barn. Continue to another stile, head down to a gate/stile and turn right along a road at Llwyn Franc (Frank's Grove).**

(8) **After about one quarter of a mile go over a stile on the left and head down following the waymarks via several stiles and through a small wood to reach a footbridge spanning a gully. Go over a stile and head straight across the next field to pass left of a clump of trees. Now join a track leading on beside a fence. Go hrough a gate and head towards a large barn, keeping the fence on your right. and shortly you will rejoin your outward route which will take you back to Llanfihangel Crucorney. On reaching the village a visit to the Skirrid Inn is highly recommended.**

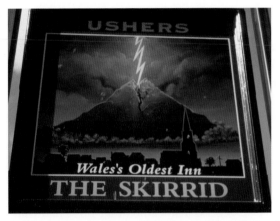

'The long spinal cord of the mountain rises steeply for a whole mile hardly ever wider than thirty or forty feet and narrowing to ten or twelve. Finally it comes to an abrupt termination northwards in a kind of notch or hook in tghe skyline which the up-reared back gives it its singular character.'

H.J. Massingham 1952

ROUTE 13
Mynydd Pen-y-Fal (Sugar Loaf) from Llwyn Du

7.5 km (4.6 miles) and 396 m (1298 feet) of ascent

'This mountain, when viewed from different points, presents a variety of appearances. It is seen to be a sharp ridge from the opposite side of the Usk, and from the south-easterly direction, it presents to the eye the form which gives it its name, a cone or sugar loaf.'

John White 1877

START: Llwyn Du car park GR 288166 (OL13)

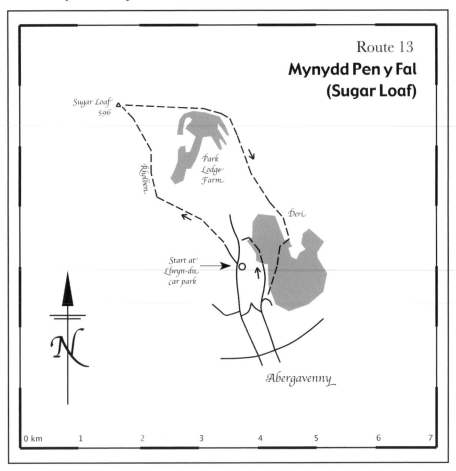

ROUTE DIRECTIONS

(1) **Follow the lane on the left leading to Porth-y-parc farm and continue through the farmyard. Before long the conical summit of the Sugar Loaf will be seen ahead. Follow a broad track between hedges to cross a stile, then go on beside a fence and over another stile.** This track provides pleasant views across the Cibi Valley.

(2) **The track soon crosses an open area and another stile is reached. Just beyond it, keep left, passing the remains of a stone wall. Now cross two stiles in quick succession and continue through a gate. At the next junction of tracks keep left.**

(3) **On reaching another stile, join the Rholben ridge track at Twyn Gwyn. Keep straight on and in due course turn right to follow a path leading directly up to the top of the Sugar Loaf.**

The summit of this peak is about three hundred metres long and there is a cluster of rocks at the western end. It is an excellent viewpoint and the panorama ranges from the Black Mountains to the north, the Usk Valley beyond Crickhowell with the Brecon Beacons in the far distance; Skirrid Fawr and the rich farmland stretching east to the Malverns and the Cotswold Hills. The whole of Abergavenny with the river Usk winding its way towards the Severn Estuary can be seen. To the south is the bulky mass of the Blorenge, and on its right the impressive limestone gorge of Clydach through which climbs the A465.

The conical summit of Sugar Loaf

72

(4) **Descend the north east side of the summit by way of a stepped path and continue down to a fence above the Cibi Valley. Turn left and walk beside the fence, heading for the Deri ridge. Where the track divides, keep right and in due course join the ridge, turning right and following a broad path along its crest. Bear right at the next junction**.

From here there are good views of the 'Three Peaks' with the symmetrical Blorenge to the south, the sharp ridge of Skirrid Fawr to the east and now behind you, the conical summit of Sugar Loaf.

(5) **On reaching Allt (376m) at the end of the highest point of the Deri ridge, descend a short slope and at a track junction make an acute turn to the right. At the next junction take the second track on the left, which leads into the woods.** The track is carpeted with the long fallen leaves of countless autumns and it descends all the way with Blorenge looming in the distance.

Deri means oak and the timber from this wood was once used to provide charcoal for Llanelly Furnace in the Clydach Gorge, which was an important iron-making centre in bygone times. The bark was used to provide tanin for the leather tanning industry in Abergavenny.

(6) **The track descends through the woods. Go through a gate and then further on, opposite a bungalow, turn sharp right to pass through another gate. Now follow a broad track through the trees.** It is a dog-leg section but provides very pleasant walking with the Cibi heard tumbling through the valley below, on its way to join the Usk.

(7) **Continue through another gate. The path narrows, rises slightly and then descends to join a farm lane. Turn left and follow the lane back to the car park**.

'It looks like a piked ridge from the opposite side of the Usk; sometimes appears in a globular shape, but at a distance, and particularly at the south-eastern side of the Skyrrid, assumes the form of a pyramid, and resembles the crater of a volcano. The cone is the highest object in the vicinity, has nothing rugged or craggy, and is characterised by smoothness and beauty.'

Archdeacon William Coxe 1801

ROUTE 14
Mynydd Pen y Fal (Sugar Loaf) from Fro
10.4km (6.5 miles) and 416m (1,331 feet) of ascent

'Whenever I see a mountain I feel I must stand on top of it and the Sugar Loaf, so clearly cut and perfectly shaped is irresistable.'

John C. Moore 1933

Start: Fro Car Park GR 291201 (OL13)

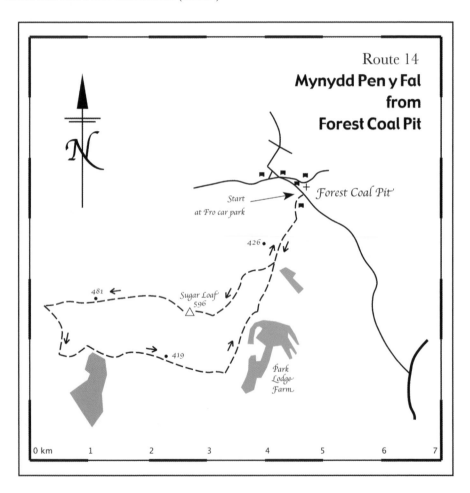

ROUTE DIRECTIONS

(1) **At the rear of the car park go through a gate and keep left beside a fence which soon becomes a stone wall. When the path divides, follow the right hand track which develops into a broad path. Go over a rise and the Sugar Loaf summit comes into view.** To the right will be seen the Gaer hill fort.

(2) **On reaching a T junction by a small cairn, go left and continue beside the stone wall, observing the craftsmanship of its construction. Skirrid Fawr will now dramatically appear on the left. After about a quarter of a mile, go diagonally right along a well worn path leading up towards some trees. Beyond the trees it steepens and then gradually brings you onto the ridge leading up to the Sugar Loaf summit. In due course the path really begins to steepen and the final ascent begins. On reaching the stone steps leading to the summikt you will know that you are nearly there. Walk along the summit plateau, touch the trig' point and admire the view.**

(3) **At the western end of the summit, scramble over some rocks and head down the Llangenny path. After about half a mile, bear left and head down the ridge to meet a stone wall. Descend to a stream at the head of Cwm Gwenffrwd and then go up the other side to reach a junction of tracks.**

(4) **Go straight across and follow a broad path that traverses around the hillside above St Mary's Vale. The track passes over a stream trickling down into the valley below and after a few yards ignore the narrow path to the left and continue along the broad one. Keep straight on at the next junction and on reaching a fence turn left beside it. Don't go over the stile but walk on with the fence on your right.** Observe how the Sugar Loaf now gradually changes its shape - becoming more and more pointed.

(5) **Soon the track dips down to cross another stream and then continues round and above the Cibi Valley. On reaching a junction of tracks, bear left along a slightly rising path which soon levels out and then descends to rejoin your outward route. This is now followed back to the car park.**

'The Sugar Loaf rises like Vesuvius, to the clouds, describing an outline remarkable for its undeviating smoothness and easy graduation.'

John White 1877

ROUTE 15
Circuit of the Blorenge

11 km (6.8 miles) and 340 m (1115 feet) of ascent

'The Blorenge reaches the very respectable height of 1834 feet, with a fine plateau several miles long sloping southwards.'

N.G. Brett-James.

START: Foxhunter Car Park GR 263106 (OL13)

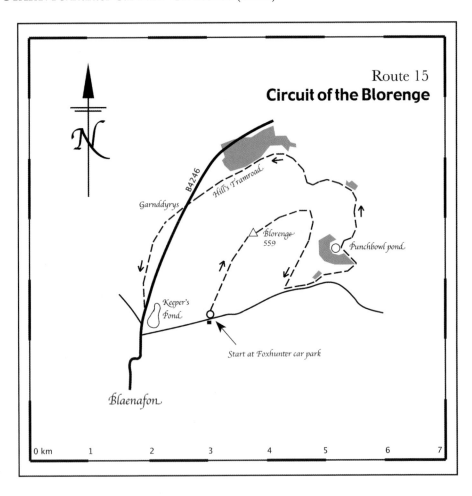

This car park is named after Foxhunter, a famous show jumping horse whose skin was buried here by its owner Colonel Harry Llewelyn. A plaque commemorating Foxhunter can be found in rocks at the end of a tarmac path leading in a northerly direction from the car park.

ROUTE DIRECTIONS

(1) **From the car park follow a well defined footpath in a north easterly direction to reach the summit of the Blorenge which is marked by a trig' point and a large cairn (559 m). Then continue in a north easterly direction to reach the edge of the escarpment overlooking Llanfoist and Abergavenny.**

(2) **Follow a wide rutted track to the right which weaves in and out of a series of hollows and humps (old quarry workings) and enjoy a new aspect towards the Coed y Prior woods. Further on the track divides. Keep on the wide path** and directly ahead on the skyline can be seen a prominent Bronze Age burial mound which is shown on the map as Carn y Defaid.

(3) **On joining the Llanellen road, turn left to follow the road down with views into the peaceful valley below. After about half-a-mile, go left by a cattle grid to cross a stile and follow a bridle path (signposted Llanfoist 3.2 km). A wide track is followed for some distance, but just before some trees, where the path descends into a sunken lane, keep left and follow a path down through the field on the left. It leads steeply down to meet a stone wall. Follow this down, treading a thick carpet of leaves, beneath overhanging trees to suddenly emerge in a very beautiful situation known locally as 'The Punchbowl'.** Before you is a pool reminiscent of a Lakeland tarn set beneath a natural ampitheatre clothed in trees. When the atmospheric conditions are right, a good echo can be obtained here by shouting with gusto at the hillside above. The Punchbowl is the site of a long forgotten quarry, where sandstone was once extracted as a source of sand for the Blaenavon Ironworks where it was used to form moulds for producing pig iron.

(4) **From the lake go up a short rise to a gate and then descend slightly through the next field, past a big heap of stones and on beside a fence. Go past a gate on the right (where a right of way leads down) and then ascend slightly, following the fence to reach another gate. Keep on beside the fence following a wide path to shortly reach another gate. A brief ascent and then the path starts to level out** and the views from here are very rewarding, providing an extensive view over Abergavenny and across to the Sugar Loaf and Skirrid Fawr. One may pick out some of the more easily identified buildings in the town such as the castle, Town Hall, St Mary's Priory Church and Nevill Hall Hospital.

The Punchbowl

View from North Escarpment of the Blorenge

(5) **Continue around the north eastern shoulder of the Blorenge and into the north facing hollow of the hill. Ignore the path ascending the steep slope above and go to the right aiming for the edge of a stone wall directly ahead. Continue along the tramroad which becomes well defined at this point.**

This is Hill's tramroad which was constructed in about 1820 to bring Blaenavon pig iron down to the Brecknock & Abergavenny Canal. It ran from the mouth of the Pwll Du tunnel to Garnddyrys Forge and then followed the 1200' contour line to the front of the Blorenge where it connected with three inclined planes descending to Llanfoist Wharf. It became redundant as a tramroad in about 1865 after the closure of the Garnddyrys Forge.

Hill's Tramroad is named after the ironmaster Thomas Hill

(6) **Continue around the northern slopes of the Blorenge enjoying a bird's eye view of Abergavenny and the Vale of Usk**. On the left you will pass the remains of a small building and then a well constructed retaining wall. It was near this point that the top incline linked up with the tramroad and here the lines of holed stones which once supported the rails are well preserved.

As you progress along the tramroad the view extends even further up through the Vale of Usk towards Mynydd Llangattock, Allt yr Esgair, Mynydd Llangorse and in clear weather the summit of Pen y Fan in the Brecon Beacons will show itself in the far distance.

Slag heap near the site of Garnddyrys Forge

Pen-ffordd-goch, popularly known as Keeper's Pond

(7) Go through a shallow cutting which leads to a tunnel, which bypassed by the track which along the top and soon dips down to the other end of the tunnel. The tramroad continues beside a leaning stone wall and contours around the hillside overlooking Cwm Llanwenarth to meet the B4246. Near here used to stand the Queen Victoria Inn which was once frequented by iron workers from Garnddyrys.

(8) Follow the grass verge of the road up to the second pylon. Then take a track passing through the remnants of a stone wall and on beside a fence to reach the site of Garnddyrys Forge where you can rejoin Hill's Tramroad. Continue along the tramroad to the head of Cwm Ifor and cross the stream where the track makes a very tight bend and then continues on around the other side of the narrow valley, past weather eroded rocks formed into intricate patterns and shapes. Soon, turn sharply left to ascend a rocky path leading through the rocks above. Looking down from here, you can see the dressed stone supporting wall of the tramroad and it is interesting to ponder on the considerable amount of labour involved in the construction of this nineteenth century transport route. The track climbs up to reach a stony track. Turn left at a corner and head up towards the wooden pylons. Now follow a grass verge on the side of the B4246 to reach Pen-fford-goch pond on the left.

This pond was constructed in 1828 and was originally known as the 'Forge Pond'. It is about 2 acres in size and was built as a header pond to increase the water supply to Garnddyrys Forge. Later, it became known as 'Keeper's Pond' after the Keeper's Cottage that used to stand nearby. This little stone cottage was demolished in about 1970. The keeper's job was to manage the Blorenge grouse moors which are the most southerly in Britain.

(9) Follow a track on the eastern side of the pond and make use of interconnecting sheep tracks to head across country in the general direction of the two radio masts. On reaching the road turn left and follow it to the Foxhunter Car Park.

'The Blorenge is interesting on many accounts. It forms a termination to the great mineral basin of South Wales, and is situated on what was formerly the Wilds of Monmouthshire.'

John White 1877

ROUTE 16
Garn Wen from Goytre Wharf

12.5 km (7.8 miles) and 315 m (1033 feet) of ascent

'From this eminence, the wild and fertile parts of Monmouthshire, the hills and dales, plains and mountains, are beautifully combined, and enriched with woodlands, which overspread the country beneath and around to a considerable extent.'

William Coxe 1801

START: Goytre Wharf car park GR 312064 (OL13)

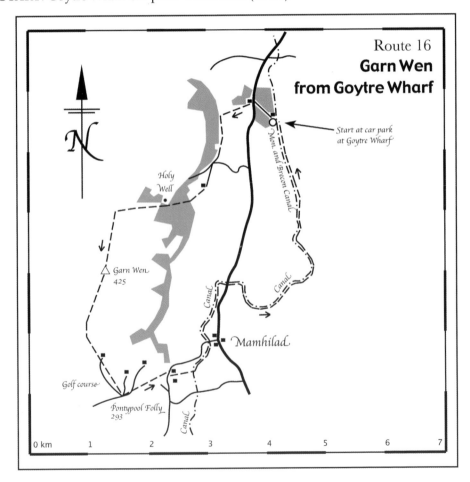

ROUTE DIRECTIONS

(1) **Walk back up the lane to reach the tarmac road. Turn left and very shortly cross the road to go over a stile. Head up a field keeping a hedge on your right to go over a stile beside a gate in the top right hand corner of the field. Keep straight on across the next field and make for a stile. Continue with a hedge on your left to cross another stile. Then walk up the next field with the hedge now on your right.**

(2) **Cross a stile to the left of a gate and turn left beside a fence. Go through a gate to pass Pen-y-stair Farm and continue along a tarmac drive. Pass through another gate, but ignore a track on the right. Descend a short way and at a junction keep straight on along the tarmac lane, enjoying pleasant views.**

(3) **On reaching the gate to Cwm Farm, turn right to follow a path beside a fence. It leads around above the cottage to another stile. From here cross a sloping field and make for a stile at the edge of a wood directly ahead. Continue through the trees with a stream babbling away on the left and follow a path gently ascending this narrow valley. Cross a stile in a fence and after a few yards the Holy Well will be seen on the left.** The Welsh name for this medieval well is Ffynnon Angaeron.

Ffynnon Angaeron - 'the Holy Well'

(4) **Continue beside the stream. Cross a stile in a fence and walk on through the trees to shortly cross the stream on a small stone bridge. Go over a stile and then bear right to follow a steep narrow path which ascends the hillside and passes a line of ancient beech trees and ascends beside a fence. Head up towards the crest of trhe ridge to join a broad track. Turn left and follow the track around the hillside enjoying the excellent view. Ignore a turning to the left. The rutted track continues beside a fence** and soon the re-constructed Pontypool Folly will come into view while the Severn Estuary may be seen glinting in the distance.

The reconstructed Pontypool Folly was officially opened by HRH Prince Charles

(5) Follow the broad track up towards the crest of the ridge. On reaching a track junction keep straight on, but in due course make a short detour to the right to take in the trig point at Mynydd Garn Wen (425m) where an extensive panorama may be enjoyed.

(6) Retrace your steps to a stone wall and continue along a path heading towards Pontypool and in due course bearing slightly right. It continues between two stone walls and to the right can be seen Pontypool Golf Course which is claimed to be the second highest in Wales. Go down to a gate and then descend into a hollow where Coed Ithel Farm nestles in a sheltered spot. Cross a stream and jshortly turn right along the access track to the farm.

(7) On reaching a tarmac road, if you wish to visit the Folly, go straight across to pass through a kissing gate and follow a path leading to the tower. After admiring the view return to the road and turn right. just before a gate, turn right by a fingerpost ('Mamhilad and Roman Road'). The path leads down to a cobbled track which descends the hillside through a tunnel of trees. Unfortunately, sections of this ancient route have been damaged by motorcyclists and horse riders. Historians disagree on the origin of this lane, some claiming that it is a Roman Road and others arguing that it is merely a medieval packhorse route connecting Mamhilad with Trevethin. However, it is of interest that a Roman coin, dating from around the third century was found many years ago, at nearby Troed-y-Rhiw farm. This stone trackway is about half-a-mile in length and substantial remnants of the cobbled surface can still be seen. At intervals, there are diagonal drains or gutters, crossing the pavement to take away surplus water.

(8) The 'Roman Road' leads down to a tarmac lane. Turn left here and shortly cross a bridge over the canal. This is the highest bridge on the B&A canal. You may wish to continue down the lane a short way to visit the Star Inn at Mamhilad, but otherwise, go right over a stile and descend to the canal towpath. Turn right to pass under the bridge and follow the towpath back to Goytre Wharf.

(9) On reaching the canal basin at Goytre Wharf, look out for a track on the right which leads down to pass beneath the canal and past a line of old lime kilns. Make your way back to the car park.

' Spirits of the past floated around me. I saw the road-makers, the shepherds, the foresters...my dreams vanished as I saw in the twilight of this canopied lane a campion in full pink bloom glowing up at me from the shadows. Did campions I wonder, grow on the banks of the Roman road as the legions passed that way ?

Fred J. Hando 1955

ROUTE 17
To the Devil's Bridge and the Lonely Shepherd

'The famous Devil's Bridge is so called because the water has worn a part of the rock beneath into the shape of a face.'

Canon D. Parry Jones 1963

9.6km (6 miles) and 290m (928 feet) of ascent

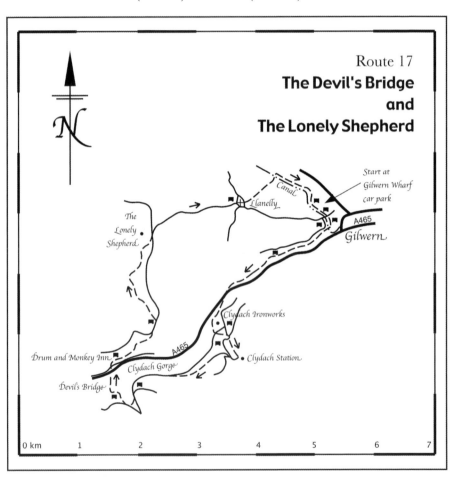

Start: Gilwern Wharf Car Park GR243146(OL13)

ROUTE DIRECTIONS
(1) From the car park follow the towpath to the left to reach the actual wharf.

Here, the Monmouthshire & Brecon Canal crosses the river Clydach on an aqueduct which was constructed in 1797. On the other side of the canal can be seen a short spur where the Clydach Wharf marked the end of the Llam-march tramroad, and the products from Clydach Ironworks were loaded onto the narrow boats for the long journey to Newport Docks.

Gilwern Wharf on the Monmouthshire & Brecon Canal

(2) Turn left down some stone steps and left again to pass through a tunnel beneath the aqueduct. Carry on past Aqueduct Cottage and by the next cottage bear left to follow a track which was once the route of the Llam-march tramroad. In due course a waterfall will be seen on the left, plunging into a black pool. Do not cross the bridge here but keep straight on beside the river, to reach Forge House.

(3) Go through a gate and along a tarmac road. Soon on the right will be seen Clydach House - sometimes referred to `as 'the house with many windows'. It dates back to the 17th century, and was once the home of Francis Lewis, clerk to the Llanelly Furnace.

(4) **Keep straight on and when joining the old Clydach road follow it uphill for a few hundred yards, making use of the pavement to reach a small gate on the left. Steps lead down to a subway passing beneath the A465 and then follow a track which leads you down to a stone bridge over the river Clydach.** This is Pont Glas which was built in 1795 to carry the Llam-march tramroad. **Go through a gate on the right and follow a track leading to Smart's Bridge (on the left).** This cast-iron bridge was built in 1824 to carry a tramroad linking the ironworks with the Clydach Railroad. **Cross the bridge to reach the site of the Clydach Ironworks.**

Established in about 1795 to take advantage of local supplies of iron ore, coal and limestone, this works remained in production for about 65 years. The site was excavated in 1987 by Blaenau Gwent Borough Council.

(5) **Now continue up the incline on the right and at the top go across the road to follow a tarmac path which leads above some houses, to reach Clydach village. Turn right at the road junction to pass a terrace of cottages where ironworkers an quarrymen once resided. Go up the hill a short distance and then turn left along a footpath to pass Troed-y-Rhiw cottage. The path soon enters the wild glen of Cwm Dyar. Go over a wooden footbridge spanning a tumbling stream and ascend a leaf-carpeted track winding up the slope above.** It is particularly picturesque here in the autumn and in spring this secluded valley echoes with birdsong and water music. Soon ahead through the trees will be seen an impressive seven arched stone viaduct which once carried the Merthyr, Tredegar & Abergavenny Railway.

This line had a life of one hundred years and its construction was a remarkable engineering achievement for not only were there steep gradients to contend with but two sets of tunnels and several viaducts had to be constructed as well. It finally fell to the Beeching axe in 1958.

(6) **On reaching the old railway track** (now a cycle path, pause to look at the large abandoned limestone quarry and then **turn right to pas the Old Railway Inn and the stationmaster's house at Clydach Station.** At the next junction, look to the left to see Nazareth Chapel, once known as 'Cuckoo Chapel'. It was licensed for marriage ceremonies which used to be performed here for couples arriving by train for their weddings.

(7) **Cross the road and keep straight on, following the cycle path to reach a point where the railway emerges from a tunnel on the left.** In 1877 the line was doubled and a second adjoining tunnel had to be built. **Keep following the cycle path, enjoying fine views across the deep gorge, to reach the Gelli Felin tunnels.**

Smart's Bridge is made of cast iron and was erected in 1824

The remains of Clydach Ironworks, as photographed in 2008

The Devil's Bridge

The cycle path turns right here to cross a bridge and follows the route of Crawshay Bailey's tramroad.

(8) Just past a long stone cottage, turn right to descend a steep flight of steps, and follow a path descending into the depths of the Clydach Gorge. The peaceful sound of rushing water mingles with the noise of heavy traffic on the road above. **At the bottom of the gorge the river is crossed on the 'Devil's Bridge'.**

If you stand in the middle of the bridge and look down into the murky depths and use your imagination, you may be able to make out the face of the Devil in a rock beside the waterfall; hence the reason for the name of this bridge.

(9) Go up a flight of steps on the other side of the bridge to reach a stile and a subway leading beneath the A465 (Heads of the Valleys Road). Turn left and continue past the 'Drum and Monkey Inn' to reach the old Black Rock road directly above. Go straight across (with care) to follow a track which soon ascends past old limestone quarries. The path roughly follows a line of electricity poles and takes you up to a tarmac road.

The Lonely Shepherd is also known as the Peakey Stone

This is the route of Crawshay Baileys's tramroad which was built in about 1830 to transport limestone from the Llangattock quarries to the Nantyglo Ironworks.

(10) **Just past a cottage turn left up a wide stony track** and ahead on the skyline will be seen a remarkable pillar of limestone which is known locally as the 'Lonely Shepherd'. It is also sometimes referred to as the 'Peakey Stone', which comes from the Welsh 'Carreg Bica', meaning the 'pointed stone'. A rock behind 'the shepherd' is said to be his dog.

The legend is that the shepherd was very cruel to his wife and for his misdeeds was turned into stone and compelled to stand on the hillside overlooking the valley for evermore. However, on Midsummer night, the shepherd resumes human form and makes his way down to the valley searching for his wife. Just like all stories of this nature, the stone shepherd must return to his mountain perch before daybreak. Years ago superstituous people used to coat the 'Lonely Shepherd' with whitewash, once a year, so that he could be seen more clearly on his annual walk.

(11) **Follow a stone wall on the right to pass below a lonely hillside cottage and then, leaving the wall continue along a well defined track, passing below the Lonely Shepherd. Then walk down beside another stone wall to reach a road junction. Go straight across and follow the road down hill to reach Llanelly Church**.

Llanelly Church is dedicated to St Ellyw or Elli, one of the many daughters of Brychan, the fifth century ruler of this area. The church stands within a circle of ancient yews and was probably a sacred spot in pre-christian times.

(9) **Directly below the churchyard follow a path which leads down into the valley to meet the Monmouthshire & Brecon Canal. Cross the stone bridge and follow the towpath to the right to reach your starting point at Gilwern Wharf**.

'The Lonely Shepherd is held in much affection by people, and hundreds visit every year. By some he is regarded as the Shepherd of the Vale and they say that once a year - on midsummer's night, he goes through the vale counting his sheep.'

Canon D. Parry Jones 1963

ROUTE 18
Craig y Cilau Nature Reserve

9 km (5.6 miles) and 320 m (1049 feet) of ascent

'I looked down into the deep misty valley of the River Usk and into the villages of Llangattock and Crickhowell, far below. Over the valley rose hill after hill; in every direction Wild Wales reared up on end in vast sweeping contours..'

Walter Wilkinson 1948

START: Park Road (oposite the Horseshoe Inn), Llangattock village.
GR 213177 (OL13)

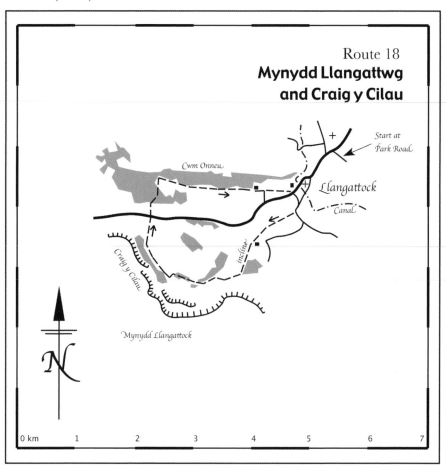

ROUTE DIRECTIONS

(1) **Walk back to the T junction and turn left to follow the road uphill.** You will be very much aware of the craggy escarpment of Mynydd Llangattwg which dominates the skyline' ahead. **Ignore the turning to the right signposted 'Beaufort'.**

(2) **Continue past the square chapel and follow the road over a canal bridge.** Observe the lime kilns on the right. They are reminders that at one time Llangattock was a very busy place, with Bailey's coal wharf and the Brecon Boat Company operating a healthy trade in coal, lime and limestone. **When the road bends to the left, go right over a stile to follow the route of a 19th century tramroad.**

(3) **Go through a gate and continue along the track enjoying the peace of this pleasant valley.** A rippling stream may be heard and in the autumn the colours can be quite spectacular. **Go through another gate and the track continues through another gate and past a cottage. Pass through another gate and cross a stream on a bridge. Keep the fence on your right to reach a stile in the corner of a field.**

(4) **From here an incline goes steeply upwards. As you ascend** look out for the occasional stone with a neat hole drilled into it, to secure the iron saddles that once held the tramroad rails in place. This ascent is steep - in fact very steep, but your efforts will be rewarded with a magnificent view. At the top of the incline you will find traces of a wheel pit where the horizontal brake wheel was once housed. Nearby is the site of the brakeman's shelter. Across to the right is a wooden seat that has been erected in memory of Brian Raymond (1948-1993) who no doubt was a regular visitor to this spot.

(5) **After admiring the view, take a deep breath and head up the next stage of the incline.** On reaching the top you will find evidence of another wheel pit.The inclines were operated with four full trams weighing approximately five tons each descending the downward rails while they pulled empty ones up an adjoining set of rails. The connecting chain ran around a turn-table at the top of each stage of the incline. A groove cut by the passage of the chain can be seen where it passed over a block of stone on the lip of the top incline.

These inclines were constructed in 1814 by the Brecon Boat Company and were later taken over by the Bailey brothers who built the tramroad from Llangattock to Nantyglo to transport limestone for use as flux in their great ironworks. It was in use up until about 1865.

View from 'Windy Corner' into the Craig y Cilau Nature Reserve

The Llangattock Tramroad contours the hillside above Craig y Cilau

(6) **Turn right along the old tramroad**, and as you walk, enjoy one of the most spectacular views in South Wales, towards Crickhowell, Table Mountain and the Pen Allt-mawr ridge of the Black Mountains. **Soon the track narrows and the slope below becomes much steeper**. Down in the valley, the rushing waters of the Onneu-fach will be heard. In places the tramroad has fallen away, leaving just a narrow path. **However, on reaching 'Windy Corner' the track widens again as you enter the Craig y Cilau Nature Reserve**. A notice board on the left provides some interesting information relating to the reserve. It was established in 1959 and is 157 acres in size, and is situated at an altitude of between 274m and 457m. It is noted as the site of some rare trees which include large and small leafed limes and four indigenous species of Sorbus. Two of these are not known outside Powys. One of them is the lesser Whitebeam (Sorbus Miniba) which is closely related to the Mountain Ash or Rowan.

Some extensive cave systems are also to be found in the Reserve including Ogof Agen Allwedd which at one time was the longest cave system in Britain (with a single entrance) and it has more than eighteen miles of passage. This claim has been superseded and the record is now held by a cave in Yorkshire, but cavers in South Wales are optimistic that one day three major cave systems inside Mynydd Llangattwg will be linked together to form a system more than 28 km (eighty miles) in length.

Just beyond a small bay in the cliff is one of the five entrances to a cave known as Eglwys Faen (Stone Church). It is a round hole in the cliff face, reached by a short scramble, which can be very slippery in wet weather. Around the corner, a steep track leads up to a larger entrance which gives immediate access to a large cavern. This is the most suitable entrance for a brief visit by a non-caver.

(7) **Continue along the tramroad and after about 300 metres look out for a narrow path descending on the right. It passes along the crest of a little ridge and gradually drops down into the valley. Bear left where the path divides to shortly pass through trees. The track now becomes more rocky and crosses a boulder strewn slope and then leads down to the left hand side of a mire called Waun Ddu (Black Bog). By the remains of a stone building follow the track up to a fence and ascend the slope above.**

(8) **On meeting a cart track, go left beside a stone wall. Descend to the Beaufort Road and go straight across to a fingerpost. Now head down to a stile. Continue through the next field and make for a gate in the bottom right hand corner. Walk on through the trees and down to the right to emerge from the wood opposite Cwm Onneu Farm. Go right past a ruined barn to reach a stile at the end of the field.**

The 'Trademan's Entrance' to Eglwys Faen

Waun Ddu (Black Bog) is a Site of Special Scientific Interest

(9) **Continue through the next field, keeping the fence on your left, go over a stile - cross a short field - go over a stile - cross a field - go over a stile. Now follow a rutted track, which soon becomes more defined and leads on between hedges. It then curves around the next field. Follow the waymarked path leading above Cilau Farm to join a lane.**

(10) **Follow the farm drive to reach a stile on a bend and cross the next field to reach a stile in the bottom left hand corner. Cross the next field to a stile and then turn left along a road.**

(11) **Walk over the canal bridge and go immediately right to join the towpath, which leads under the bridge. Continue past the massive bank of lime kilns at Llangattock Wharf,** where the Llangattock Boat Club have their moorings.

(12) **Immediately before the next bridge go right and follow the road downhill and continue back to your starting point.**

'Above the tram road are steep cliffs; below it a precipitous slope leads down to the wooded stream where buzzards nest in the trees.'

C.H.D. Cullingford 1950

ROUTE 19
Mynydd Llangynidr

14 km (8.75 miles) and 190 m (623 feet) of ascent

'A little further southward the monstrous hulks of the Mynydd Llangynidr and the Mynydd Llangattwg black the horizon...'

H.J. Massingham 1950

START: Car park near Blaen Onneu GR 157171 (OL13).

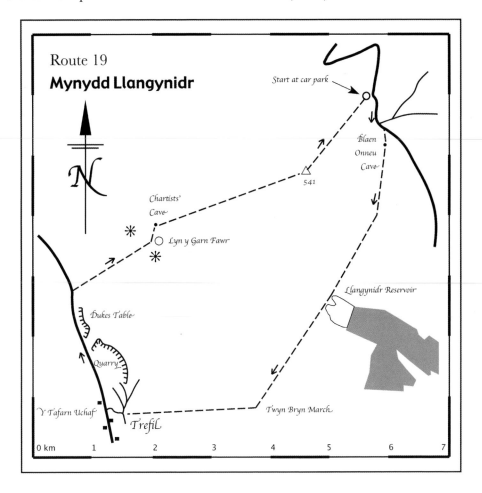

The Duke's Table, near Trefil

The Chartists' Cave on Mynydd Llangynidr

NOTE: *This route is not recommended on a misty day unless you are competent at mountain navigation. It will provide the walker with a map and compass exercise even in clear weather and can be dangerous for unskilled navigators in poor visibility, who could spend the remainder of their lives wandering around in endless circles.*

ROUTE DIRECTIONS

(1) **Follow the B4560 south past the junction with the road leading to Crickhowell and shortly turn up a track on the right which leads toan abandoned quarry, which contains the Blaen Onneu caves**.

(2) **From here head across country, following occasional sheep tracks, towards Llangynidr Reservoir. As you come over the crest of the ridge the reservoir will be seen directly ahead. Make for the western end of the reservoir (end opposite the dam) and descend into Cwm Odyn-ty to cross the feeder stream. Then head up the other side and cross the moor in a south westerly direction to reach Twyn Bryn-march (472m)**.

(3) **From here go west to descend into Cwm Milgarw, avoiding bogs where possible and make for the village of Trefil, where Y Tafarn Uchaf (formerly the Quarryman's Arms) is available for refreshment.**

(4) **Continue along the road in a northerly direction for about a mile and look out for the Duke's Table on the left, below the road and near a stream (GR 114141).** It consists of a low circular grass bank with a small mound in the centre. During the 19th century it was used as a lunch stop by the Duke of Beaufort's grouse shooting parties.

(5) **Now head across the moor in a north-easterly direction to find Llyn y Garn fawr.** This is an obvious lake after periods of heavy rain but in the summer it is very often dry. **To the north of here is the famous Chartists' Cave which can be quite difficult to find (GR 127153).**

Although the entrance is about 2 metres high, the cave is easily missed, being concealed in a hollow. Inside is a chamber providing excellent shelter and two passages that can be explored by suitably equipped cavers, lead to further caverns within the cave. It is reputed to have been used by the Chartists in the 19th century as a meeting place and an ammunition store, prior to their historic march on Newport in 1839. Their story is dramatically told in Alexander Cordell's well known novel *Rape of the Fair Country*.

(6) **Now head for the unnamed trig' point (541m) and from there make a bee line back to the B4560 and your car.**

ROUTE 20
A Bird's Eye View of Llangorse Lake
04 miles) and 830m (2722 feet of ascent)
Length if following alternative route: 21.18km (13.24 miles)

'Far below me, Llangorse Lake, some five miles in circumference, sparkled amid a foreground of woods, meadows and homesteads which glowed with the peculiar richness imparted by the slanting sunlight of an afternoon in late September.'

A.G. Bradley 1903

WARNING: After heavy rain the first part of this route may be flooded, in which case you will need to walk along lanes via Llanfihangel Tal-y-llyn to Talyllyn and Pennorth where the main route can be joined at Llangasty Village Hall. This alternative route involves a road walk of 4 miles (6.45km).

START: Park near the public toilets on Llangorse Common GR 128273 (OL13).

The Welsh Crannog Centre with Allt yr Esgair in the distance

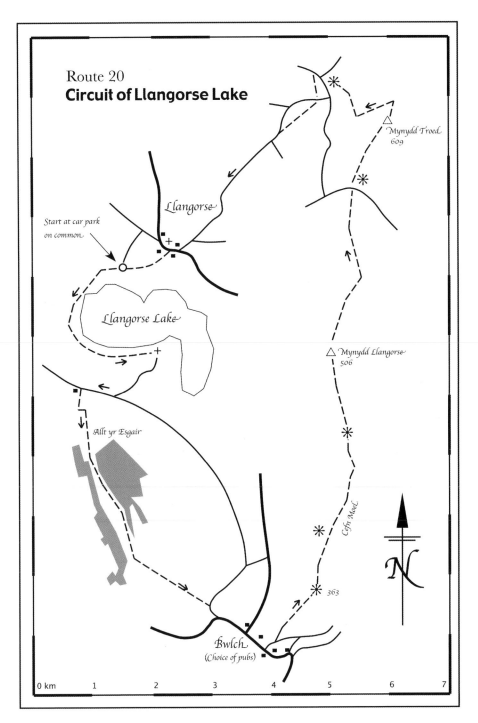

Route 20
Circuit of Llangorse Lake

Mynydd Troed
609

Llangorse

Start at car park
on common

Llangorse Lake

Mynydd Llangorse
506

Allt yr Esgair

Cefn Moel

363

N

Bwlch
(Choice of pubs)

0 km   1   2   3   4   5   6   7

This walk provides an opportunity not only to visit Llangorse Lake, but also to complete a circular hill walk linking the summits of Allt yr Esgair, Mynydd Llangorse and Mynydd Troed which provide quite outstanding panoramic views.

ROUTE DIRECTIONS

(1) Walk in a westerly direction across the common to reach a footbridge spanning the Afon Llynfi.

There is a local belief that the water in this river, flowing into the lake from the south, does not mix with that of the lake, nor do the fish in the river pass into the lake. Instead, they swim with the river which flows out of the lake on the other side and on to the River Wye.

(2) If the field is not flooded (see the Warning on page 102)), go through a gate and then diagonally left to cross a field to reach a kissing gate. Cross the next field to reach a gate at the end of a stone wall. Head across the next field, passing two pollarded oaks and bearing slightly right to coss a stream on a footbridge. Bear slightly right through the next field to reach a board walk and a gate. At the track junction keep straight on. The building directly above is Ty Mawr Farmhouse which dates back to Elizabethan times. **The path continues via more kissing gates to reach Llangasty Nature Reserve (where a path to the left leads down to a bird hide on the edge of the lake). Go through a gate on the right and then on beside a fence to rteach a long section of board walk. Then through more kissing gates to reach a lane leading right to Talyllyn Church.**

(3) After visiting the church follow the lane up to a T junction and turn right to reach Llangasty Village Hall where a Bridleway fingerpost directs you to Allt yr Esgair (the ridge with the wooded slope). Go through a gate and follow the green lane. This leads up to the foot of the ridge. On reaching a junction turn left.

(4) At the next set of gates go through the hunting gate in the middle to follow the crest of the ridge. The track is an old Roman road and it provides a sheltered route between high banks giving a welcome break from the wind on a gusty day.

The Romans liked to build their roads along high ground for they no doubt wished to avoid problems of ambush in the wooded valleys wherever possible. From Allt yr Esgair the Roman road led to Pennorth and then turned westwards to where the line of the present-day A40 passing near the 'Old Ford Inn' at Llanhamlach.

Gaining height steadily, you will shortly enjoy an excellent view of Llangorse Lake (Llyn Syfaddan). This is the largest natural lake in South Wales and it was created during the last Ice Age when an extension of the ice which moved down the Wye spilled southwards into the Usk along the Llynfi valley. Eventually this tongue of ice retreated and a moraine was formed in the area between Llanfihangel Tal-y-llyn and Talgarth. This barrier resulted in surface water collecting until it overflowed to form the River Llynfi which flows northwards to the Wye.

In shape the lake is not unlike a boot of which the sole points due south and the upper part west. In the centre it is 15 metres deep and there is a long standing tradition that the Roman city of Loventium lies beneath its waters. They say that it was drowned because of the wickedness of the inhabitants. It is possible that this legend is really based on an artificial island in the lake known as a crannog, and constructed of posts, rubble and earth.

Excavations between 1989 and 1993 by the National Museum & Galleries of Wales and Cardiff University have revealed that this artificial island was the site of a royal palace for the ruler of Brycheiniog. Examination of the well preserved timbers contained in the construction has shown by tree-ring dating that they were felled between AD889 and AD893. It is recorded in the *Anglo Saxon Chronicle* that in AD916 Aethelflaed, Lady of the Mercians sent an army into Wales and they destroyed *Brecenanmere* (a reference to Llangorse Lake) and captured 'the king's wife and thirty-three other persons.' The king in question would have been Tewdwr ap Elise who no doubt had the crannog constructed.

A dug-out canoe, hewn from a single oak log, was discovered in 1925 in mud at the bottom of the northern part of the lake and it has been associated with the island. It can be seen in Brecon Museum, and there is a replica near the Welsh Crannog Centre, adjoining the lake.

Llangorse Lake abounds in a wide variety of fish, from pike of impressive size to eels so long that there is a saying, 'Long as a Syfaddan eel'. Not surprisingly the lake is a Site of Special Scientific Interest. Water always attracts large numbers of people and Llyn Syfaddan is under enormous recreational pressure for it attracts fishermen, sailors, water-skiers, picnickers, walkers and ornithologists.

This lake has alway been famous for its birds and it was claimed by the chronicler, Giraldus Cambrensis in the twelfth century, that the birds here will only sing for the rightful ruler of Wales.

Llangorse Lake from Allt yr Esgair

View from the summit of Allt yr Esgair towards the Brecon Beacons

(5) **Go through another hunting gate and follow the fence. Take a track on the left and continue straight up, following the path along the crest of the ridge.** On the summit is an outcrop of rock which provides a very fine vantage point with good views across the Usk Valley towards the Brecon Beacons. The descent now begins.

(6) **The path leads down to a gate and there is a fine view of the Black Mountains to the left. On this section the narrow path leads down between hedges and is sometimes very muddy for it is regularly used by pony trekkers. In due course you will emerge onto a road.**

(7) **Turn right and follow the lane to reach the A40. Turn left and follow the road with care, using the pavement on the left in due course. Head up through the Bwlch Pass.** There is a saying in these parts that 'once across the Bwlch (Pass) a Welshman never returns.' During the stormy years of border warfare such a belief was probably quite appropriate.

Bwlch was a borough in the lordship of Blaenllynfi and the scanty remains of a castle (on private land) hide in trees on the north-west side of the village. Leland in 1522 described it as a 'very fair castle, now decaying.'

(8) **Turn up the lane beside the old post office and after a few hundred yards turn left at a junction. This leads towards a white cottage. Go through a gate just above the cottage and follow a track beside a stone wall to join the ridge above.** To the left can be seen Allt yr Esgair and Llangorse Lake while to the right you look past the wooded Myarth to Sugar Loaf and Blorenge.

(9) **A well defined track now follows a fence and wall along the crest of the ridge.** If it is clear you will see on the skyline, the white trig' point on the summit of Mynydd Llangorse. **The path snakes along the crest of the ridge with good views on either side. It divides not far from the summit. Bear left to reach the trig' point.** From here on a clear day the view is quite breathtaking.

Looking westwards over Llangorse Lake the Brecon Beacons stand proud with Pen-y-Fan and Cribin particularly prominent, while beyond this range the northern escarpment of the Carmarthen Fans may be seen. Looking northwards the view takes in the Radnor hills and on a clear day Plynlimmon may also be seen.

(10) **Continue along the crest of the ridge and soon Mynydd Troed will be seen in the distance. Descend the end of the ridge, enjoying a fine view of Llangorse Lake. The path zig zags down to a col. Ahead now looms the daunting steep slope of Mynydd Troed. This is optional of course!**

107

View of the Brecon Beacons from the northern end of Mynydd Llangorse

'Now I strongly recommend the mountain (Mynydd Troed). It is only some 2,200 feet high, but it stands out sharply from this group of the Black Mountains.'

A.G. Bradley 1903

(11) On reaching the road, pause to examine the Macnamara boundary stones and then cross the road and go through a gate. About a hundred metres up the slope of Mynydd Troed, ahead of you on the right, can be seen a Bronze Age burial mound. **The steep ascent is made all the more interesting by a series of false summits, but at last you reach the trig' point (609 m).** This is also a fine viewpoint, with Pen-y-Gadair Fawr in particular, dominating the skyline to the east, crowning the mass of the Black Mountains.

(12) Now either return down to the col and turn right, to follow lanes down to Llangorse village, or if you are feeling more adventurous, follow the ridge down in a northerly direction for a short way. Then descend the west side to pick up a path slanting diagonally down the slope. In due course leave this path and head straight down to the left end of a stone wall that can be seen below. You will reach a small boundary stone which is inscribed 'Macnamara 1821'. Opposite and by the end of the stone wall cross a stile.

(13) Walk down a broad track between a fence and a stone wall. Follow the track down keeping the fence on the right. Go over a stile in the top corner of the field and on through the trees to join a tarmac road. On reaching a bend bear left along a cart track, walking between hedges. Look out for a finger post on the left by a gate. Go through this gate and walk straight across the field to a gate and then on through the next field to pass between farm buildings. Walk through a farmyard and turn right down a road which leads you back to Llangorse village.

(14) Just before Llangorse Church and opposite the 'Old School', go through a gate between a house and a stone wall. Cross a stile and follow a path through fields, via two gates to reach a footbridge spanning a stream. Go straight across the next field to a stile and he end of the walk.

On returning to your starting point near the lake you may be interested in visiting the Welsh Crannog Centre which consists of a viewing platform and reconstruction of a roundhouse thus interpreting the man-made island in the lake.

The western slopes of Mynydd Troed gave us a beautiful sight of Llyn Safadan, lying like a sheet of silver in the cup of the now broadening valley.'

E. Elliot Stock

ROUTE 21
Tor y Foel

8 km (5 miles) and 410 m (1344 feet) of ascent

'He is no true mountaineer who only cares for technical difficulties, and anyone who has the true love of the wild hills in him will certainly find plenty of healthy amusement among the mountains of Breconshire.'

R.G. Sandeman 1938

START: Coach and Horses Inn Car Park at Llangynidr GR145198 (OL13,) but seek permission before leaving your car here.

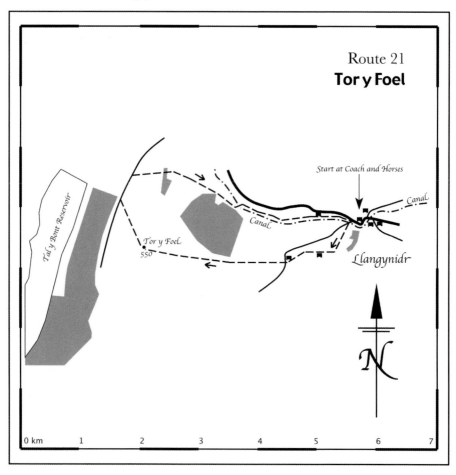

Tor y Foel from the river Usk

ROUTE DIRECTIONS

(1) **Cross the road bridge over the canal. Turn left and shortly go through a gate on the left to follow the canal towpath. On reaching some locks, go left over a footbridge and keep straight on, following a path ascending through the trees to reach a stile. Continue through the trees looking down into the narrow Crawnon valley. On emerging from the trees cross another stile. Now go straight across the next field heading for a stile in a gap in the hedge. Tor y Foel will be seen rising up to the right. Cross a stile and head up, bearing right to a stile in a fence to the left of a gate.**

(2) **Head diagonally right across the field to reach a stile and continue through the next field to a gate. Cross the lane and go over a stile directly opposite. Head straight up the field to a stile in the top right hand corner. and continue up the next field to a gate. Shortly, go through another gate and head for the farmhouse to join a tarmac lane. On reaching a T junction go straight across and pass through a hunting gate to follow a shady track between hedges, leading up to the ridge of Tor y Foel.**

(3) **Go through a hunting gate and then up to a stile.** Pause here to catch your breath and admire the view which takes in the Usk Valley, the Black Mountains and Sugar Loaf. **Then continue with the track threading its way through the bracken.** Soon far below on the right, the Usk will be seen snaking down through

the valley with the ridge of Allt yr Esgair behind it. **On ascending the next rise, Tor y Foel summit appears to come into view. But as you will shortly discover, this is one of those hills which has several false summits that fool you into a premature state of satisfaction. You will pass over a number of humps before at last you arrive at a point where the only way on is down.** But first stop and admire the superb view from the summit cairn (551m).

Directly ahead may be seen the whale back mass of the Brecon Beacons and the ring of hills that surrounds you is only broken to the north by the Valley of the Usk. In the far distance can be seen the hills of old Radnorshire.

(4) Descend the northern slope of Tor y Foel to reach the road far below and at a point just before a cattle grid turn right and follow a rising track and shortly bear left at a junction to reach a gate. Cross a sloping field towards a wood. Go through a gate and walk through the next field and descend to a rutted track. Continue along a broad track beside a fence to reach a gate/stile.

(5) Cross a field to reach a gate at the corner of a wood directly ahead. Shortly afterwards, cross a stream and bear right across the next field to go through a gate. Then follow the path leading to a gate and then down towards the canal. turn left to join a track leading down to the canal. Cross a bridge and a stile on the right, giving access to the canal towpath which is then followed back to Talybont.

'The Brecknock & Abergavenny Canal is one of the most beautiful canals in Britain. Its course is almost entirely within the Brecon Beacons National Park and follows the Usk Valley with superb views across its surrounding country.'

R. Alan Stevens 1974

ROUTE 22
Cwm Claisfer and Cwm Crawnon

20 km (12.5 miles) and 570 m(1869 feet) of ascent.

START: Village car park at Llangynidr, directly opposite public toilets on B4558 GR 155196 (OL13)

NOTE: *This route is not recommended for walking in summer when the bracken is high for the paths in the upper part of Cwm Claisfer are then very difficult to follow.*

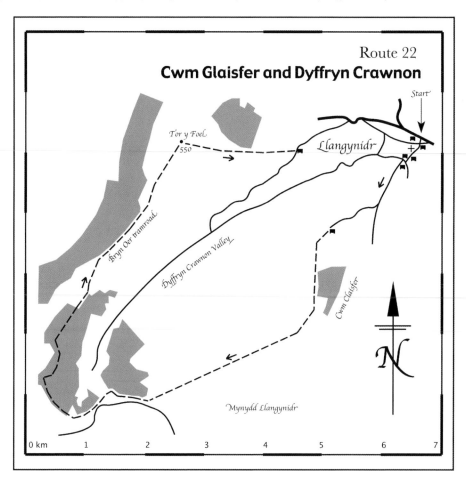

Route 22
Cwm Glaisfer and Dyffryn Crawnon

ROUTE DIRECTIONS

(1) **Walk up the road past Llangynidr Church**, which was founded in the 6th century by St. Cynidr, a grandson of King Brychan of Brycheiniog. **On reaching a junction take the road leading up into Cwm Claisfer, passing Pen yr rheol cottage on the right and a chapel graveyard on the left.**

(2) **Follow the quiet lane for a couple of miles, and just before it makes a sharp turn over a bridge go through a gate on the right. A cart track is now followed through gates, across fields and past the remains of an old metal barn, to reach one built in stone. Continue along the track above the barn and before long the track becomes narrower. Walk on between stone walls and past a ruined building to reach a stile. Ahead will now be seen a disused waterworks building beside the Nant Claisfer.**

(3) **Continue up the valley, following a path on the right bank of the stream. This is a very pleasant valley decorated with a series of small waterfalls. It becomes necessary to ascend the bank on the right and in due course the source of the Claisfer is reached by a lone tree.**

(4) **Walk on through an area of limestone boulders, and on across the lonely wilderness of Mynydd Llangynidr, with the Claisfer now but a murmuring memory behind you. Before long the summits of the Beacons will come into view. Head down to the Trefil road and join it near the junction with a track which descends into Cwm Pyrgad. Turn right along the tarmac road but shortly leave it to follow the old Bryn Oer Tramroad which runs beside a fence above a forestry plantation**. (The name Bryn Oer, meaning cold or exposed hill) has been corrupted to Brinore). To the left are the now silent Trefil quarries while on the right one looks down into the deep wooded valley of Dyffryn Crawnon and its handful of little cottages and farmhouses.

The Bryn Oer Tramroad was once an important link between Tredegar and Talybont-on-Usk and was constructed in 1815 for the purpose of transporting coal and lime from Bryn Oer (Cold Hill), on a twelve mile journey to a wharf on the canal at Talybont. Here the cargo of coal or other materials was transferred into horse-drawn narrow boats and conveyed to Brecon. Countless tons of coal must have been transported along this impressive route when Brecon was an important coal distribution centre for this part of Wales. As you walk along the tramroad you will notice stone sleepers which once supported the L-shaped plateways along which the loaded trams travelled. They were pulled by horses who were harnessed one behind the other. An average 180 tons per week were transported by the Rhymney Ironworks Company until about 1864 when it went into decline.

Cwm Claisfer

View into the Duffryn Crawnon Valley

The Bryn Oer Tramroad

Bryn Oer Tramroad Marker Stone
(Brinore is an anglicised version of Bryn Oer)

(5) The old tramroad is followed around the head of the valley and further on it bends around into a side valley at a point known as the 'Horseshoe Pass'. Eventually it emerges from the trees and the views open up once more as you pass Pen Rhiw Calch which is the site of an inn where the hauliers used to stop to quench their thirst.

(6) On joining a track above the Talybont Reservoir continue along the ridge with Tor y Foel looming ahead. At a narrow point on the ridge, at the base of Tor y Foel, leave the road to go through a gate on the right, where a tarmac lane leads down to Bwlch-y-Waun Farm. It descends into the valley along the side of Tor yr Foel.

(7) On reaching a road go straight across and follow a lane past a farmhouse to go through a gate. Below now can be seen Llangynidr village. Follow the waymarked path down through the fields, crossing several stiles on the way, and descend through some trees to reach a footbridge over the canal.

(8) Turn right along the canal towpath and follow it to the Coach & Horses Inn. Turn right beside the inn , up 'Castle Road' and on reaching a junction bear left. Follow this road to reach a T junction. Go straight across and follow a short narrow lane back to your starting point.

'When we reach the mountain summits we leave behind all things that weigh heavily on body and spirit down below. We leave behind all sense of weakness and depression. We feel a new freedom, a great exhilaration, an exaltation of the body no less than of the spirit. We feel a great joy.'

J.C. Smutts

Winter ascent of Pen y Fan

THE BRECON BEACONS

'The Brecon Beacons reach high in heaven in Pen y Fan and Corn Du, the indigo corniced throne of an intriguing moorland.'

Tudor Edwards 1950

Most people who visit the Brecon Beacons for the first time are surprised to see such a dramatic and shapely skyline when they drive along the A40 towards Brecon. Dignified and majestic the north facing escarpment of the Brecon Beacons towers above the Usk Valley and it is this particular range of hills that gives its name to the National Park.

Writers in the eighteenth century sometimes referred to the highest peak (Pen y Fan) as Mount Denny. This was probably due to a misunderstanding of the Welsh language. Even today people visiting the area often say Pennyfan instead of 'Pen u Van', so one can appreciate how the mistake arose. Other writers of the same period proclaimed the highest beacon to be Cadair Arthur and thus began yet another Arthurian legend. The heroic king was portrayed as a giant, whose head soared above the clouds and was encircled by a rainbow. The back of his chair was a semi-circular sweep of two or three miles and the seat was marked by Llyn Cwm Llwch.

Today, most people take the name Brecon Beacons for granted, and are unaware of the fact that it dates back to the time when a complex warning system consisting of a chain of intervisible hill beacons was established. Their use can be traced back to the time of the start of the troubles with France in the fourteenth century, when cross channel raids made the threat of invasion a constant worry. News of the approaching enemy would have been conveyed along the coast and inland by a series of fire signals.

Where the terrain was suitable, the gap between the beacons was about six to eight miles and a chain of beacons included a high point which would be visible from a wide area and no doubt Pen y Fan would have been used for this purpose.

It is recorded for example that beacons were fired along the Cornish coast on the sighting of the Spanish Armada. However, once the Armada threat was removed, beacons lost their importance for several hundred years.

At the beginning of the nineteenth century, when Napoleon threatened to invade this island, beacons were again manned, and it is recorded that in 1804, the beacon at Hulme Castle in Berwickshire was accidently lit, causing a long chain of beacons to be set off, bringing out hundreds of volunteers to arms.

The jubilee of Queen Victoria was celebrated in 1887 with the lighting of many beacon bonfires throughout the country and again in 1897 for her diamond jubilee. A beacon was fired on Pen y Fan on both these occasions. On 31 December, 1992 a beacon was lit on the summit of Pen y Fan to celebrate the new European unity and the advent of the single European Market. Thousands of beacons were lit on this night throughout the twelve EC countries and spectacular firework displays held on the summits of hills and mountains.

Many walkers on their first visit to the Brecon Beacons often think of them as small hills for the name 'Beacons' certainly gives that impression. However, it should be remembered that Pen y Fan the highest peak in South Wales is only 199m lower than Snowdon. It should also be emphasised that although grass covered and easily accessible, particularly from the A470, the Brecon Beacons still demand the respect that must be accorded to other areas of high peaks and steep escarpments. However inviting the day may be, one should not approach the Beacons carelessly.

During the last four decades, the Brecon Beacons have suffered from erosion caused by an ever increasing number of visitors and the more popular paths became wider and deeply rutted tscars on the landscape. The central part of the Beacons is owned by the National Trust and during the last two decades they have worked hard on an ambitious programme of footpath and erosion repair to arrest the decline. Employing the traditional technique of 'pitching' once used by the Romans considerable progress has been made in repairing the damage and the full time staff and volunteers are to be congratulated on the work they have completed to date.

Classic view of the Brecon Beacons skyline from the A40

ROUTE 23
Pen y Fan by the Traditional Route

8km (5 miles) and 500m (1650 feet) of ascent.

'Gradually the clouds lightened and lifted; the peak of Pen y Fan, or Arthur's Chair, showed but a few hundred yards off and two or three hundred feet higher, and I lost no time in getting on top of the highest point in South Wales.'

A. G. Bradley 1903

This is the shortest and quickest way to the summit of Pen y Fan, the highest mountain in South Wales, from the A470, which is one of the highest trunk roads in Britain, but by no means the most interesting route.

START: Pont ar Daf layby on the A470 GR 988199 (OL12). Here there are toilets, plenty of parking space and the occasional ice cream van in good weather.

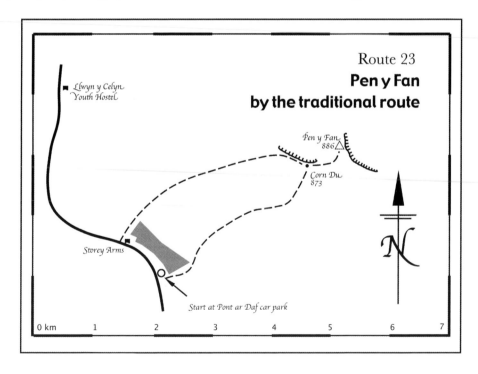

(1) **About 50 metres south of the toilets follow a track on the left to pass between two conifer plantations. Go through a kissing gate and then descend to cross a stream (Blaen Taf Fawr) on a footbridge.** Continue up the obvious path, which has been much improved in recent years by National Trust working parties who have laboured hard to provide drainage and repair erosion problems. Forty minutes of steady walking brings you to the col of Bwlch Duwynt (Pass of the Black Wind), the saddle between Duwynt and Corn Du (Black Horn).

The track to Bwlch Duwynt from Pont ar Daf

(2) **Now follow a track to the left around the right flank of Corn Du**. Directly below is the Taff Fechan valley and the Upper and Lower Neuadd Reservoirs. These are the highest of the Beacons reservoirs. Soon you will reach the col between Corn Du and Pen y Fan. **Ascend the final slope to the summit of Pen y Fan (886m or 2906 feet).** The actual top is no longer marked by a trig point which has been replaced by a cairn following an archeological dig.

Care must be taken on this summit, as on all the northern Beacons escarpments, because of the near-vertical 200 metre north face. The view ranges from the Black Mountains to the Preseli Hills of Pembrokeshire and from Exmoor to Plynlimon. Westwards, beyond Fan Fawr, stands Bannau Brycheiniog, highest point in the Carmarthen Fans. Llyn Syfaddan (Llangorse Lake) is to the north-east and Cadair Idris in Snowdonia, may reveal itself far to the north-west in exceptionally clear weather.

View from summit of Corn Du towards Pen y Fan

View towards Cribyn from summit of Pen y Fan

'The vapours that sometimes invest the Beacons are so dense, that the traveller is in danger of falling over its precipitous side.'

Thomas Roscoe, 1862

(3) Return to the col and ascend to the summit of Corn Du which is also marked by a cairn. A burial mound excavated here some years ago was found to contain a stone cist which the experts dated at about 2000 BC. **From here walk in a north-westerly direction, descending with care the ridge of Craig Cwm Llwch. It is steep at first but becomes more gradual in due course.**

(4) Follow a track to the left and descend to Blaen Taf Fawr (a stream). On the other side ascend and go slightly left to reach a ladder stile crossing a wall. Carry on uphill and at a path junction bear left. Follow this path down hill towards Fan Fawr and it will bring you down to Storey Arms.

Storey Arms is at the highest point of the A470 and the name originates from an old inn which stood about 300 metres to the south. Once owned by a wealthy landowner, Anthony Storey-Maskelyne, it closed in 1897.

When the existing building was in use as a Youth Hostel, the South Wales Region of the YHA, proudly boasted that this was the highest Youth Hostel in England and Wales. In the 1970s it became an Outdoor Activity Centre and the replacement Youth Hostel was established at Llwyn-y-celyn a couple of miles down the road towards Brecon.

(5) Turn left and follow the edge of the main road with care to reach the car park at Pont ar Daf.

'We then walked along the ridge to the second and higher triangular summit, peeped with nervous dread on my part over the almost perpendicular precipice towards Brecon, noted the exact correspondence in slope of the two summits, and then back to the ridge and a little way down the southern slope to where a tiny spring trickles out - the highest source of the river Taff - and there lying on the soft mountain turf, enjoyed our lunch and the distant view over valley and mountain to the faint haze of the Bristol Channel. '

Alfred Russell Wallace 1846

ROUTE 24
Cwm Llwch Circuit

7 km (4.37 miles) and 575 m (1886 feet) of ascent

'Reaching Llyn cwm llwch we had lunch by the frozen waters. The ice was of great thickness and told of the severe conditions of this record winter.'

R.G. Sandeman 1937

START: Car Park in Cwm Llwch GR 006246 (OL12)

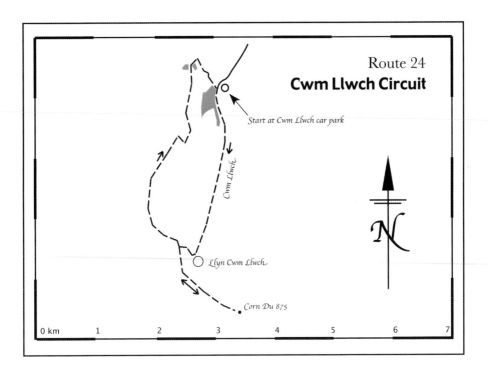

ROUTE DESCRIPTION

(1) **Follow the track to pass around the old Cwm-llwch Farm which is used by Malvern School as a weekend mountain base. Climb two stiles in quick succession and follow the track uphill. After about 400 metres the track starts to climb steeply over a hump and then leads more gradually towards the high circular hollow below the flat-topped summit of Corn Du. Where the track divides take the lower one which leads directly to Llyn Cwm Llwch.** For the unsuspecting walker the surprise comes at the last minute. Immediately below the looming slopes of Corn Du the scene is suddenly peaceful and inviting, for here is a small mountain lake of glacial origin. It is almost surrounded by the mound of a moraine.

Llyn Cwm Llwch is a small mountain lake of glacial origin

The famous chronicler Giraldus Cambrensis described this mountain pool as a mysterious spring which rises in the Brecon Beacons, 'deep, but of square shape like a well, and although no stream runs from it, trout are sometimes said to be found in it.' It is in fact a corrie lake, left behind when glacial ice receded from the north facing cwms of the Beacons.

Years ago, it was known as the lake of Cwm-llwch dingle and also Pwll-y-doctor (the doctor's pool) after a famous scholar, Dr David John Rhys, who once lived in the old farmhouse further down the valley.

According to local tradition the pool is supposed to be bottomless. However, in the 1970's students from Hereford College of Education plumbed it from a floating lilo and found it to be about 15 metres deep in the centre. Many years ago it was claimed that Mr. Jenkin Price - Recorder of Brecon once tied the bell ropes of Llanfaes Church together and dangled them with a heavy weight attached into the pool, but he failed to touch the bottom.

(2) From the pool ascend a track on the right steeply up through a series of zig zags to reach the ridge of Craig Cwm Llwch and before long you will come to the Tommy Jones obelisk, a memorial to a small boy who in August, 1900, ventured too far from Cwm-llwch Farm where he was staying with his grandfather. Despite a search lasting several weeks the missing boy was not found and it was even feared that he might have drowned in Llyn Cwm Llwch. It was also suggested that he had been kidnapped.

The 'Daily Mail' offered a reward of £20 to anyone who could solve the mystery. It was solved on Sept 2 of that year, when a local man on a Sunday afternoon walk discovered Tommy's body on the ridge above the pool at a height of 2250 feet above sea level. None of the searchers had considered it likely that the little boy would have wandered so high and only the valley had been searched. The man who found poor Tommy contributed his £20 reward towards the cost of the inscribed memorial stone which was erected in July of the following year.

The inscription reads:

This obelisk
marks the spot
where the body of
Tommy Jones
aged 5 was found.
He lost his way
between Cwmllwch
farm and the Login
on the night of August 4th 1900.
After an anxious search
of 29 days his remains
were discovered Sept 2nd.
Erected by voluntary
subscriptions.

W. Powell Price
Mayor of Brecon 1900

The obelisk provides a useful landmark in misty weather and it enables you to accuately pinpoint your position on the ridge. However, if you are using an old map it is important to know that in recent years the National Trust moved the obelisk about 50 metres closer to the edge of the ridge. The boots of countless walkers had eroded the ground around the pillar causing it to lean at quite an angle.

(3) **This route is intended as a short circular walk, but one may make a deviation to the summit of Corn Du by continuing up the ridge. At first it ascends gradually and then quite steeply for the last section. In a strong wind it is advisable to keep clear of the slopes on the left. dropping steeply into the cwm, for a sudden gust may blow you off balance.**

(4) **Assuming you have returned to the obelisk, now follow the path down the ridge to reach Pen Milan and then bear right down a broad green track which descends like the 'Cresta Run' to lower ground.** This track was once used by quarrymen to bring slabs of rock down from a quarry on the hillside above. **Walk on threading your way between clumps of gorse with the little white Cwm llwch cottage to be seen below on the right.**

(5) **Follow the rutted path across scrub land towards a white building and on approaching it, keep left of the fence and descend into the valley below. Go down to a gate in the bottom corner of the field. Beyond the gate follow a track beside a stream, shortly ford it and after about 100 metres, by a house, cross the stream and go over a stile on the right.**

(6) **Cross the field keeping the fence on your left to reach a stile. Continue straight across the next field to a stile beside a gate. Walk on with a fence and then a wall and farm building on your right. Pass around the front of the building and then go across the next field bearing slightly left to reach a stile. Walk across the next field to another stile and cross yet another field to reach the Cwm Llwch track. Turn left and follow it back to the parking area.**

'The view from Corn Du, the first of the Beacons which stands 2863' above sea-level was tremendous, embracing on one side all the sweet loveliness of the Brecon pasture-lands, with their infrequent, whitewashed farmsteads, and on the other side range after range of wild moorlands stretching as far as Carmarthenshire.'

S.P. Mais 1939

ROUTE 25
Llanfrynach Circuit

17 km (10.6 miles) and 600 m (1968 feet) of ascent

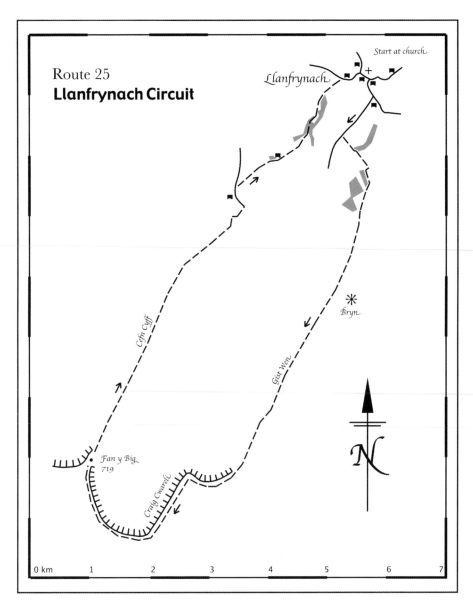

Route 25
Llanfrynach Circuit

Start at church

Llanfrynach

Bryn

Cefn Cyff

Gist Wen

Fan y Big
719

Craig Cwareli

N

0 km   1   2   3   4   5   6   7

START: Llanfrynach village. Park near public toilets, opposite the church.
GR 075257 (OL12)

The village church is dedicated to St Brynach who was confessor to Brychan the 5th century King of Brycheiniog. It has an interesting tower but the greater part of the building was rebuilt in 1855. Inside are memorials to the de Winton family.

(1) Facing the toilets, turn left, then shortly turn right and after a few hundred metres turn right along Tregaer road which is followed for about for nearly 1 km and then go over a stile on the left to follow a cart track between hedges. Go through a gate and walk down to a ford. On the other side follow the track around and up the left hand side of the field to reach a finger post.

(2) Turn right and go over a stile beside a gate and then turn immediately left to follow a path ascending through the trees. It curves right for a while and then heads straight up to a stile beside a gate, Head up to the open hillside and the Bryn comes into sight. Continue following tracks along the lower slopes of Bryn with Pen y Fan and Cribin prominently seen across to the right.

(3) The track leads up Gist Wen and via Rhiw Bwlch y Ddwyallt to reach a shallow col on the western side of Craig Pwllfa. Bear right here to follow the edge of the escarpment; taking in Bwlch y Ddwyallt, Craig Cwareli and Craig Cwmoergwm, to reach the summit of Fan y Big ('Hill of the Beak').

(4) After admiring the view and taking dramatic pictures of your companion perched on the 'Diving Board', follow a broad track steeply down the nose of Fan y Big, and then pleasantly along the ridge of Cefn Cyff, to eventually reach a stony track which leads down to a road.

(5) Follow the road downhill and look out for a fingerpost on the left directing the way to Llanfrynach. Go through a gate on the right to follow a path across a field, bearing slightly left to reach a stile. From there walk down a rutted track with a fine view of the Black Mountains ahead of you, to reach a gate.

(6) Cross a lane and go over a stile directly opposite. Walk across the next field keeping the hedge and fence on the left. Go over a stile and turn right along a farm track which is followed around the left-hand side of the next field. Cross a stile and follow a broad rutted path through the next field. Just before a stream, turn right along the bottom edge of a field, where the right-of-way has been legally diverted.

The 'Diving Board' on Fan Big

(7) **The track drops down to a point where the stream joins the river. Turn left here, go through a hunting gate and cross the stream. Continue through the next field with the river now flowing on the right. This final section makes a very pleasant finish to the walk. Pass through a hunting gate and walk on beside the river. Ascend a short slope and continue through the next field to go through a gate. Follow the broad track with the river now flowing noisily on the right.**

(8) **Continue pleasantly through the trees, crossing the next field and then over a stream. Keep straight on to reach a stile. Then go through a kissing gate and turn right along a lane. Take the next turning on the right which leads past Tyfry, a 17th century farmhouse**. On the other side of the road is a building which once served as a water-powered timber mill. This explains the purpose of the leats and channels recently passed that were built to convey water to drive the mill wheel. **Follow the lane back to Llanfrynach and your starting point**.

The two peaks of Mounchdenny Mountain (Pen y Fan) now present themselves in a different direction. They may also be said to personify ubiquity. The one is more pointed than the other; but both enveloped in clouds, communicate a grandeur to the prospect, which compensates in great measure for its poverty and want of beauty.'

Benjamin Heath Malkin 1803

Corn Du, Pen y Fan and Cribin

ROUTE 26
Fan Big and Cribin

13 km (8 miles) and 605 m (1984 feet) of ascent

'I climbed the Arete of Bryn Teg, and when about halfway up espied two people standing on the summit of the reigning peak.'

W.A. Poucher

START: Cantref Church, but parking is limited GR 056255 (OL12)

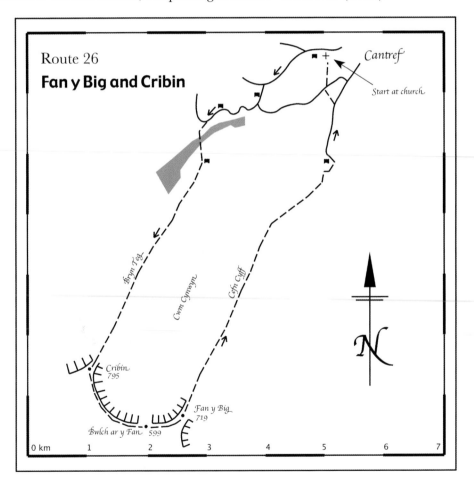

ROUTE DIRECTIONS

(1) From the church follow the road uphill, ignoring the turning to the right. Then take the next turning on the left, signposted 'Brecon'. Ahead now can be seen the NE face of Pen y Fan and the snout of Cribin. Go left at the next junction and then on past Pontbrengarreg farm. Keep straight on downhill at the next junction.

(2) Cross a bridge and turn right to follow the road beside the river Cynrig and at the end of the lane continue through a gate and follow a stony track between high hedges. In due course the track curves around to the right. Go through a gate and on between the hedges. Ignore the gate and track on the right at the next bend. On meeting a tarmac road, continue straight on up the Roman Road. Pen y Fan can now be seen directly ahead and Fan Big stands proud across to the left. Soon a gate gives access to the open hillside.

(3) Take the track which leads up to the ridge of Bryn-teg (Fair Hill) and heads straight for the summit of Cribin. It is fairly easy going until the infamous 'snout' is reached, rising steeply for the final 100 metres to the top.

The steep 'snout' of Cribin with the north east face of Pen y Fan behind

This sharp arête is an obvious feature of the Beacons skyline when viewed from a distance at certain angles and has led some writers to describe Cribin as the 'Welsh Matterhorn', a nickname it shares with Cnicht in Snowdonia. It is a steep scramble but the view from the crest is a just reward.

'Tackle the steep ridge ahead. This is continuously steep and the going is hard for the time being, but on reaching its summit the rewards are immense.'

W.A. Poucher 1962

(4) **Descend Craig Cwm Cynwyn to the 'Roman Road' and then continue up the steep slope ahead to reach the summit of Fan y Big.** This is a fine viewpoint and a projecting rock slab known as the 'diving board' provides a dramatic photograph if you have a willing model with a good head for heights! **From here descend the ridge of Cefn Cyf in a northerly direction, for a couple of miles, to reach a stony track descending between tumbled stone walls. It leads down to a tarmac lane which is followed downhill.**

(5) **Ignore the footpath to the right. At the next bend in the road, go over the second of two stiles on the left. Follow the left hand edge of the field to reach a stile beside a gate. Continue down the next field, keeping the hedge on your left.** Cantref Church can now be seen nestling in the valley below surrounded by trees.

(6) **In the bottom left hand corner of the field go over a stile beside a gate. Turn right along a tarmac lane. Shortly go over a stile on the left (signposted 'Cantref Church'). Head down through the next field keeping on its left hand side. Go over a stile in the hedge and walk across the next field to reach a stile. Descend stone steps on a bank and turn left down an ancient sunken lane. It leads down to a ford which can be avoided by crossing a stile on the right beside an old stone building. Cross a field to reach a footbridge and rejoin the lane which leads up to a road. Turn left and walk back to the start.**

'The mountain slopes were greener than usual from recent rains, the ruddy precipices of Cribin and Pen y Fan were quite fiery in the sun's rays.'

A.G. Bradley 1914

ROUTE 27
Tour of the Talybont Valley

20 km (12.5 km) 730m (2336 feet) of ascent

'These Talybont hills seem to draw more cloud than the Black Mountains and some really magnificent mist effects can be enjoyed on them.'

R.G. Sandeman 1947

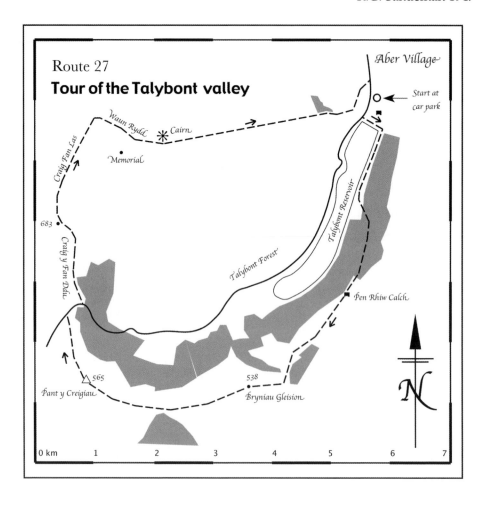

Route 27
Tour of the Talybont valley

The Talybont Valley contains the beautiful Talybont Reservoir, which is fed by the Afon Caerfanell and was built between 1895 and 1927 to provide Newport with a plentiful supply of water. Flooding the valley destroyed 25 farms and 2875 acres of land were compulsorily purchased. It is a good location for observing waterfowl and other aquatic wildlife. The valley is also known locally as 'the glyn' or Glyn Collwn: after the ancient site of Capel Glyn Collwn which stood a mile beyond the reservoir.

START: From car park just below the reservoir dam. Toilets and camp site. GR 105208 (OL12).

ROUTE DIRECTIONS
(1) Walk up to the road, turn left and shortly go left again over the dam. On reaching the end of the dam, turn right to follow a tarmac lane which runs just above the reservoir and provides pleasant views across the water.

This reservoir was created to supply water to Newport in the 1930s by damming the small Caerfanell river. In 1974 it was designated as a Local Nature Reserve, mainly on account of the wildfowl it attracts in winter.

The lane becomes a cart track which ascends to provide excellent views across the valley. In due course it passes beneath a disused railway line which once connected Brecon with Merthyr and was known affectionately as the 'Best and Most Respected Railway' (BMR). Alternatively it was often referred to as the 'Breakneck and Murder Railway'. There was a 7 mile gradient of 1 in 37 from Talybont to the top of Glyn Collwyn. At Torpantau the tunnel was 609 metres long and at an altitude of 400metres (1,131 feet) the highest in Britain and it took two years to build. The line opened in January 1863 and closed one hundred years later.

(2) Ignore the next track on the right and on reaching the next junction take the left hand of two rising tracks. Keep straight on at the next junction.

Looking down on the reservoir now, the full length of it may be seen and across the valley will be noticed a prominent cairn known as Carn Pica which will be visited towards the end of this walk.

In the 1950's much of the land in this valley was leased to the Forestry Commission. They mainly planted conifers but the existing broadleaf trees were preserved wherever possible. Japanese Larch, Norway Spruce, Douglas Fir and Scots Pine were planted on the lower slopes while Sitka Spruce were introduced to the higher exposed land.

(3) **A track is joined which leads up to the ridge and shortly crosses the route of the Bryn Oer Tramroad** which was opened in 1815 to carry coal and lime from Bryn Oer, near Tafarnaubach, Tredegar, to the canal at Talybont. Look out for the remains of a stone building on the left at Pen Rhiw-calch. This used to be the 'Rock Inn' where thirsty tramroad hauliers once stopped to enjoy quarts of ale.

Talybont Reservoir

(4) **Follow the wide track along the crest of the ridge, enjoying views of the Black Mountains on one side and the Brecon Beacons on the other. Snaking around a rocky shelf cut into the side of the hill the track leads up to a pass known as Pen Bwlch Glasgwm. Now leave the track and head in a westerly direction across the open moorland of Bryniau Gleision and make for the trig' point on Pant y Creigiau (565m).** From here is a good view of Pen y Fan, Corn Du and Cribyn, while below in the valley can be seen the Blaen-y-glyn waterfall. It sometimes freezes in winter and makes a very impressive photograph.

(5) **Descend to the edge of the forestry plantation on the right. Cross a gravel track and on reaching the tarmac road go straight across and follow a well trodden path which leads up to Craig y Fan Ddu. In due course it crosses a stream and then descends into a gully. Go up the slope on the other side and then tackle the final section of steep track to gain the ridge above.**

(6) **Follow the path, keeping the valley on your right and in due course it will be necessary to cross the rocky gully of the Caerfanell**, which in spate is an impressive cascade into the valley below.

Across the valley below the left end of a line of cliffs is a memorial cairn which marks the location where a Wellington bomber crashed whilst on a training exercise on the night of 6 July 1942. It was piloted by Sergeant J.B. Kemp with a crew of five Canadians. Flying from the Midlands they encountered dense cloud over the Beacons and struck the edge of Waen Rydd, scattering wreckage over a wide area. The crew all died in the crash and were buried at Hereford. Their names are inscribed on a plaque fastened to the cairn which was erected in 1980 by the Outdoor Activity Group of Tredegar Comprehensive School, led by Peter Jones, a well known local historian.

The path leads along the edge of the escarpment of Craig Fan Las and at last the edge of the north escarpment will be reached at a narrow col. From here there are fine views to the north, while to the west may be seen the north-east face of Pen y Fan with the snout of Cribin rising in front of it.

Memorial cairn and wreckage of the Wellington bomber

Carn Pica is a prominent cairn which has been restored in memory of John Inns

(7) **Turn right along a track crossing a wide expanse of peat hollows, often referred to as the 'Moon Country'. The track dips in and out of the peat hollows formed by decayed plants that grew here thousands of years ago. On reaching the plateau of Waen Rydd, follow a broad track with Sugar Loaf and the Black Mountains to be seen in the distance. Make for Carn Pica, a large cairn on the eastern edge of the plateau.** Talybont Reservoir now lies directly below, perhaps sparkling in the sunlight.

(8) **A steep descent leads down Twyn Du, and at the end of the ridge, continue with a wall on your left to follow a stream down to a stile. Walk on beside a fence with the stream now on your right. The path crosses the stream and then leads down to a tarmac lane which is followed down to a road. Turn right and your starting point is not far away.**

'Talybont Reservoir is more than just another earth fill dam and unlike some of those who built it and who suffered because of it, and can recall the events of 1920-1940, there is a saga to narrate.'

David Tipper 1992

ROUTE 28
The Beacons Grand Circuit

22 km (13.75 miles) and 840 m (2755 feet) of ascent

'The north east face of Pen y Fan, in winter conditions as prevailed that morning, looks every inch an Alpine peak.'

R.G. Sandeman 1938

START: Pont ar Daf layby on the A470, GR 988190 (OL12).

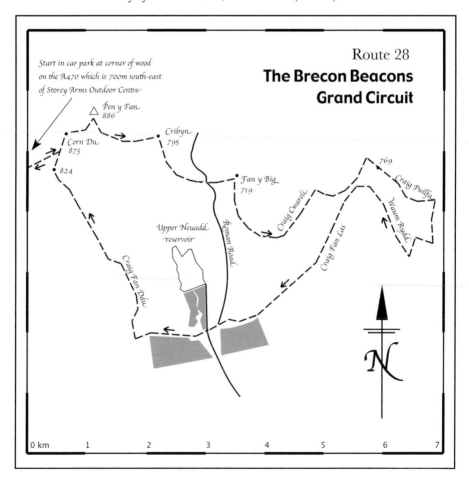

ROUTE DIRECTIONS

(1) About 50 metres north of the toilets follow a track on the left to pass between two conifer plantations. Go through a kissing gate and then descend to cross the Blaen Taf Fawr on a footbridge. Continue up the well trodden path and about forty minutes of steady walking will bring you to Bwlch Duwynt, the col between Corn Du and Duwynt.

(2) Follow the path to the left and scramble up rocks to the flat summit of Corn Du (Black Horn) where a Bronze Age cairn was excavated a few years ago. In the valley below looking like a giant's tear drop is the small and mysterious pool of Llyn Cwm Llwch. This corrie lake was left behind when glacial ice receded from the north facing cwms of the Beacons and according to local legend it is bottomless. **Descend ENE to a col and then follow a broad eroded path to the summit of Pen y Fan** (Top of the Peak) where another Bronze Age cairn has been excavated and the now much missed trig' point, unfortunately removed in the process.

The view from Pen y Fan (886m) on a clear day is particularly impressive. Westwards beyond Fan Fawr and the moorland of Fforest Fawr stands Bannau Brycheiniog the highest peak of the Carmarthen Fans, which is sometimes referred to as the Black Mountain. Cader Idris, the highest mountain between Pen y Fan and Snowdon may reveal itself far to the north-west in very clear weather. One may also see the Preseli Hills of Pembrokeshire and Dunkery Beacon on Exmoor, giving an outlook over no less than four National Parks. On the far side of the Usk Valley are the Black Mountains, a compact group of ridges and valleys which provide opportunities for solitude and walks offering extensive views in all directions.

(3) Leaving Pen y Fan's windswept summit head down Craig Cwm Sere to descend a rocky stepped path which has been constructed by National Trust volunteers in their sterling efforts to combat erosion. Drainage channels have been laid and the surface improved with stones laid in jigsaw fashion, involving considerable labour, patience and skill. Take care in the wet for this stone path can be very slippery. On reaching a col overlooking Cwm Sere you are now faced with a steep ascent to the summit of Cribin (The Summit) - sometimes referred to as the Welsh Matterhorn - an exaggerated title it shares with Cnicht in Snowdonia.

Pause to catch your breath and look back at the gully seamed north-east face of Pen y Fan. These are the highest Old Red Sandstone mountains south of Scotland. They were formed from the sand and mud of a great moraine estuary which covered this area in Devonian times, about 300,000,000 years ago.

The tops of the Beacons are capped by 'plateau beds' of Old Red Sandstone giving the peaks their characteristic 'table top' appearance. The summit of Cribin, however is quite narrow and drops dramatically to the north where the ridge of Bryn Teg reaches towards Brecon.

Bwlch ar y Fan, known as 'The Gap', through which passes the reputed 'Roman Road'

(4) **Descend Craig Cwm Cynwyn to Bwlch ar y Fan, popularly known as 'The Gap' (599m) where a reputed Roman road crosses at this point.** This ancient route may well have linked the Roman forts of Dol y Gaer in the south and Y Gaer to the west of Brecon. It was certainly the original Cardiff to Brecon route and was not superseded until the Turnpike road via Merthyr and Storey Arms was built. It now forms part of a recreation route known as the 'Taff Trail' which links Cardiff with Brecon and is particularly popular with mountain bikers.

(5) **From the 'gap', climb eastwards to the summit of Fan y Big (719m). The slope is steep but not as long as the approach to Cribin. (A pony path goes off to the right, by-passing the summit and providing a more gradual approach to the ridge).** The summit of Fan y Big is a fine viewpoint and is marked by a small cairn. Notice the projecting rock known as the 'diving board'. It provides a good opportunity for a dramatic photograph (see page 131).

(6) **Head south-east again over Craig Cwm-oergwm. Towards the east can be seen the 'moon country' of Gwaen Cerrig-Llwydion.** An old quarry is soon reached; its rocky depressions provide useful shelter for a refreshment stop.

(7) **Continue along the path around the horse-shoe shaped valley with the track following the edge of the ridge. On turning a corner Llangorse Lake and the Black Mountains come into view. Follow the ridge, now in a north-easterly direction, to the end of the next curve, where the track starts to descend. Leave the main track here and cut off to the right, heading for a cairn on the skyline about a mile away (769 metres). From the cairn make for the next spot height (762 metres).**

(8) **Continue to the east (facing the distant Sugar Loaf) to reach a large cairn.** This is known as Carn Pica and it marks the end of the summit plateau. In the distance can be seen Talybont Reservoir with Tor y Foel standing behind it.

(9) **Head south along the blunt end of Craig y Fan, following the track on its edge overlooking a narrow valley below (Cwm Tarthwyni). At the end of this ridge, turn west. The return journey now begins.** Below is the afforested valley of Cwm Cynafon. Swing around a tight corner to reach the end of Cwar y Gigfran. At the end of this ridge is the 'balcony', a large block of sandstone which provides a sheltered resting place and vantage point.

The 'Balcony' is a fine vantage point

(10) **Continue north-westwards along the ridge. The path is well defined, but take care because there is steep ground below. On reaching the final section of cliff,** look down to see a cairn erected as a memorial to the crew of a Wellington bomber, which crashed here during World War II. **Now cut back across the edge of the 'moon country' to reach the head of the valley. From here, head upwards to gain the edge of Craig Fan-las and a good track.**

(11) **On reaching a rocky gully carrying a stream, strike south-west away from the ridge to follow a path across open country to reach two cairns at Garn Fawr.** There are interesting rock formations at this point which provide useful shelter from the wind. **Continue south-west to reach a pile of rocks.** This is probably the largest area of scattered rocks in the Beacons. **From the lower end of the rocks follow a path heading in the direction of the forestry plantation on the other side of the valley.**

(12) **The path leads down to a stream and soon the reservoir buildings are in sight. A gradual descent into the valley brings you to the Roman Road, which is followed north to the Lower Neuadd Reservoir. Go through the gate and follow a right of way over a leat and then across the derelict dam. Make for a stile and walk towards the right hand end of a forestry plantation. Head up, first gradually and then steeply to gain the ridge of Craig Fan Ddu.**

(13) **The ridge is now followed northwards with fine views of the Neuadd Reservoirs. The long narrow, lonely valley of Cwm Crew is passed on the left. Continue over Rhiw yr Ysgyfarnog ('Slope of the Hare'), where the ridge narrows and Craig Gwaun Taf, to reach Bwlch Duwynt where the 'tourist path' descends to your starting point at Pont ar Daf.**

'He who rises early will imbibe the freshness of earth and sky, the scent of turf and heather, the purity of hill-air. He will hear the lambs crying from the hillsides and see mists, grey in the half-light, settled low and menacing on the hills.'

Frank S. Smythe 1941

ROUTE 29
Traverse of the Beacons

16 km (10 miles) and 800m of ascent (2624 feet)

'The Beacons stand up sharply in their grimmest and spikiest mood, the three peaks running together in a skyline like a most satisfactorily sized Welsh dragon.'

Walter Wilkinson 1948

START: Pont-ar-Daf car park on A470 near Storey Arms GR 988198 (160)
This is a linear walk requiring transport from or to each end. The best way to walk a linear route of this length is to use two vehicles or alternatively a non-walking member of the party can drive around to the finishing point to pick up the walkers at the end of the day.

ROUTE: Pont-ar-Daf - Bwlch Duwynt - Corn Du (873m) - Pen-y-Fan (886m) - Cribin (795m) - The Gap - Fan y Big (720m) - on via Craig Cwm Oergwm - Craig Cwareli - Bwlch Ddwyallt (763m) - Waun Rydd (763m) - Carn Pica (cairn) - down the ridge of Twyn Du to finish at a car park 0.5 km south of Aber and below the Talybont Reservoir dam. Toilets at car park GR 105208 (161)

View of the Brecon Beacons from Pen y Crug hillfort, north of Brecon

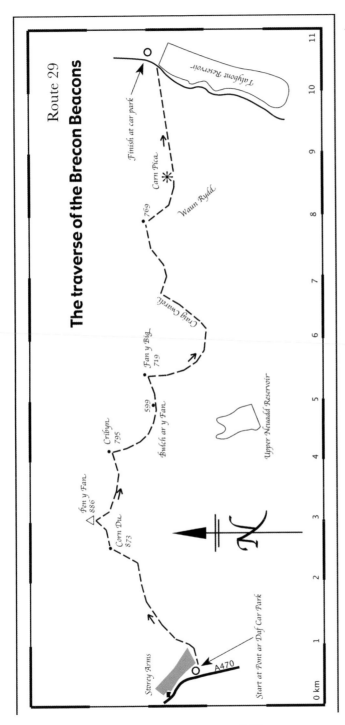

He that mounts precipices, wonders how he came there, and doubts how he shall return. His walk is an adventure, and his departure an escape.'

Dr Johnson

147

THE WATERFALL COUNTRY

'In fine weather the water is low, the rivers tame and some of the cascades invisible. To see them in perfection the traveller must wait for rain, a delay that will be amply repaid by the gratifications which the scenery must provide.'

Richard Warner 1798

Some of the most beautiful waterfalls in Britain are to be found in an area of the Brecon Beacons National Park, known as the 'Waterfall Country'. It comprises a series of wooded valleys down which flow the rivers Mellte, Hepste, Pyrddin, Nedd Fechan, Llia, Dringarth and Sychryd. These rivers drain the upland of Fforest Fawr, rising on the high plateau which slopes southward from Fan Gyhirych, Fan Nedd, Fan Llia and Fan Fawr. First cutting their way through Old Red Sandstone, these rivers proceed through Carboniferous Limestone, Millstone Grit and the Coal Measures, to combine near the village of Pontneddfechan (sometimes Anglicised to Pontneathvaughan) and form the River Nedd, which then makes its way down to Neath.

This is a fascinating area to explore, with impressive waterfalls, moss covered boulders, wooded slopes, curious rock formations and intriguing cave systems. The waterfalls have a breathtaking beauty that cannot be found anywhere else, even in Wales. Each fall has its own individual shape and form. Varying in height and width, some display water falling in one majestic lea, while in others the fall is broken by a ledge or large boulders.

After heavy rain they are particularly impressive, but a visit to these wooded valleys during a period of hard frost or heavy snow can make a very interesting expedition, which may even require the use of ice axe and crampons. Sgwd Gwladys and Sgwd Einon Gam on the Pyrddin river are generally the first falls to freeze because they face east.

A good base for exploring this area is Ystradfellte, a small village situated at an altitude of 250m (825 ft). English and foreign visitors to this village often find its name hard to pronounce and variations of their attempts range from WHYSTRADFELLTEA to EXTRA FILTHY! Try saying USTRADVETHTUR and you will be on the right lines.

The 'Waterfall Country' was once regarded as a very remote area and years ago it was not unusual to walk around the falls and hardly see a soul. But the fame of its scenery has spread and this is now an area under considerable pressure, with an estimated 200,000 visitors a year. Such large numbers unfortunately cause erosion and the National Park Authority has undertaken considerable work to improve the paths. Some have been re-routed and the use of others discouraged. A car park has also been established at Gwaen Hepste to take pressure off the one at Porth yr Ogof.

Swd Isaf Clun-gwyn
on the river Mellte

With use of some of the traditional paths no longer encouraged, many guidebook descriptions including my own *Exploring the Brecon Beacons National Park* (first published in 1980 and no longer in print), are now out of date, for some parts of the route descriptions are no longer applicable. The routes described in the book you are now reading, are up to date at the time of writing and the paths used are mostly waymarked and signposted.

It must be emphasised, as warning notices will confirm, that some of the paths are potentially dangerous for inexperienced and badly shod walkers. Sensible footwear with soles that grip well is essential, for many of the routes pass above steep drops, while muddy slopes and man-made steps can be very slippery in the wet. Children in particular should be kept under control for a slip above a steep drop, with rocky ground below can prove fatal!

For walkers who wish to visit the Mellte and Hepste falls there are several possible starting points:-

Gwaen Hepste Car Park G.R. 935125 (OL12)
This car park has been established by the National Park Authority in order to take some of the pressure off the Porth yr Ogof car park. It is reached by following the minor road off the A4059 from a point about a mile north of Penderyn. After about a mile take a left turning and a sign to Gwaen Hepste car park will shortly be seen on the left.

From this large car park a network of waymarked paths providing circular walks of varying lengths has been established by the National Park Authority. The Red Circuit combined with the Green Paths gives access to the falls on the Mellte and the Hepste.

Clun-Gwyn Roadside Car Park G.R. 918105 (OL12)
This is a small car park on the side of the Ystradfellte to Pontneddfechan road and it provides quick access to the falls on the Mellte. Follow a lane down between fences and go over a stile. Shortly, you will see a National Park information board relating to Coed Rhaidyr 'Wood of the Waterfalls'. From here the well trodden path leads on via a few stiles to the valley of the Mellte and you will soon here the sound of Sgwd Isaf Clun-gwyn.

Porth yr Ogof Car Park G.R. 928125 (OL12)
This car park is situated on a lane to the south of Ystradfellte just above the river Mellte and it is equipped with public toilets. It can also be reached on foot by a waymarked route from the Gwaen Hepste Car Park and many walkers will wish to come here to visit the impressive entrance of Porth yr Ogof cave. ROUTE 30 describes a walk starting from this location.

ROUTE 30
Mellte and Hepste Falls

'Strangers who come afar, having heard of the fame of this valley, may see but little in it, from expecting too much and in too little time; most of the beauties lie out of the direct route, and require some search.'

William Weston Young

Start: Porth yr Ogof Car Park G.R. 928125 (OL12)

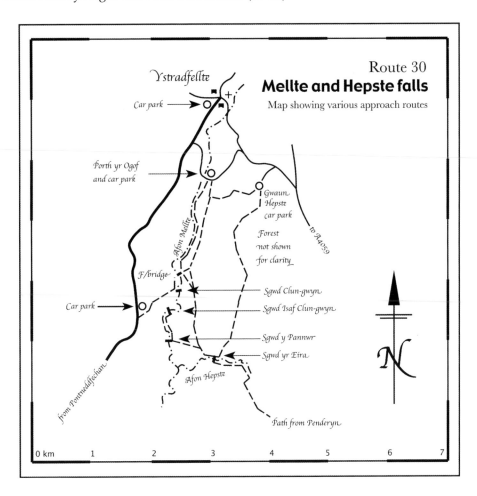

ROUTE DIRECTIONS

(1) **Cross a stile at the far end of the car park and follow a path down to a limestone gorge,** where the river Mellte goes underground through the impressive mouth of Porth yr Ogof which is 65ft (20m) wide This is the largest cave entrance in Wales, but it is not the only way into the cave, for experienced and properly equipped cavers are able to enter the underground system at no less than fifteen different points.

Porth yr Ogof has the largest cave entrance in Wales

Casual visitors wandering into the main entrance should only venture a short way without a light and the White Horse Pool is soon reached. This name stems from the calcite streak on the wall directly ahead which resembles the head of a horse. A passage on the right gives access to the main passage of the river, but it should only be entered by those properly equipped. Unfortunately, there are very few formations in the cave and the best are in Hywel's Grotto which is not easy to find and is reached by crawling and wriggling on one's stomach along low sandy passages and through pools of water.

After periods of heavy rain, the Mellte rises dramatically, and the main entrance becomes impassable, but it is impressive to watch the water surging into the cave. During exceptional conditions the water has been known to reach the roof inside the entrance chamber and large trees have been swept into the cave.

Several people have tragically been drowned in the cave and warning notices have since been erected to warn cavers of the dangers of undertaking a through trip. Any exploration beyond the entrance chamber should only be carried out by properly equipped parties led by an experienced caver.

(2) **After inspecting the entrance of Porth yr Ogof, return to the car park and cross the road to follow a signposted path on the other side along the abandoned river bed of the Mellte. Soon you will pass three pothole entrances to the cave, through which a caving ladder is necessary to descend the forty-foot drop. Continue along the footpath for another 100 metres to pass between two side openings** formed when the roof of the underground chamber collapsed long ago. They provide glimpses of the River Mellte on its underground journey. Over the top of the next rise, you come to the resurgence, where a large rock platform provides a splendid view of the dramatic water exit and the pool below. The total length of the underground river from the main entrance to the resurgence is about 300 metres and the drop in level approximately 7 metres. This resurgence is sometimes referred to as 'Death Mouth Cave' for numerous fatal accidents have occurred here.

Resurgence of the Afon Mellte at Porth yr Ogof

'A branch of the cavern is said to extend many miles in length and persons have lost their way and never returned.'

Theophilus Jones 1898

(3) **Retrace your steps a short way and go up to the rocky path above, which shortly descends the the bank of the Mellte. This is followed for about half-a-mile to reach a footbridge.** Do not cross the bridge but carry on past it following a waymarked path which leads you to Sgwd Clun-gwyn, generally referred to as the Upper Fall. Descend to a point where you can look down on the fall but take care for it is a steep drop and particularly dangerous for young children.

(4) **Carry on along the path following the waymarked route which takes you up a side valley to a fence. Follow it to the right along a high level path overlooking the Mellte Valley. In due course a signposted junction is reached where a diagonal path leads down to river level, and the falls of Sgwd y Pannwr and Sgwd Isaf Clun-gwyn.**

Although smaller than the other two, Sgwd y Pannwr (the Fall of the Fuller) is quite picturesque. The pool below the fall was once reputed to be the home of a huge fish which refused to be caught. The name of this fall is probably a reference to the foaming appearance of the water at times when the river is in spate. It is hardly likely that woollen goods were ever brought here for fulling.

(5) **Continue along the track to reach Sgwd Isaf Clun-gwyn.** Watch out along this stretch of river for dippers, which may be seen alighting on rocks and flying inches above the fast flowing water in their search for food. They are small brown birds with white throats. Mellte means lightning and the river is so-named because it rises rapidly when in flood. Sgwd Isaf Clun-gwyn (Lower White Meadow Fall) is particularly impressive after heavy rainfall

.
(6) **It is now necessary to return along the same route to regain the high level track which is signposted to Sgwd y Eira.** The view from this track is very pleasant, embracing the whole of the Mellte Valley northwards to Fforest Fawr and southwards to the Vale of Neath.

In due course you will hear the sound of Sgwd yr Eira in the distance and it may be glimpsed in the valley below. **From the wooded ridge between the Mellte and the Hepste rivers a stepped path descends steep steps to the foot of Sgwd yr Eira and leads behind the fall.**

Sgwd yr Eira is the most famous of all the waterfalls in these valleys, due to the fact that it is possible to stand behind the broad curtain of water. In very wet weather the fall may appear as a broad sheet of foam, but generally there are three separate falls. Of course the greatest prize of all is to see the fall completely frozen, but this is an extremely rare event.

Sgwd Clun-gwyn ('White Meadow Fall')

Sgwd y Pannwr ('The Fall of the Fuller')

Sgwd Isaf Clun-gwyn ('Lower White Meadow Fall')

Sgwd yr Eira (Spout of Snow) on the river Hepste

Sgwd yr Eira in winter conditions

The top of the fall is overhanging and the water is thrown clear of a rocky ledge which is about three feet wide, and provides apathway behind the curtain of thrashing water and spray. This is the only path from one side of the valley to the other and years ago farmers used to drive their sheep along this route. Below the fall the Hepste passes through a spot known as the Devil's Glen and it is the setting of eerie tales about ghosts, fairies, goblins and witches.

(7) Return up the long flight of steps to regain the upper track and turn right. After about 100 yards turn left to follow a waymarked path leading up through the trees. After a short ascent, turn left at the next main junction to follow a broad track which leads on through mixed woodland. Keep straight on at the next signposted junction. Go over a stile beside a gate and continue to reach a secluded farmhouse. Follow the diverted path between a stone wall and a fence, passing below the farmhouse and rejoin the main track at the end of the stone wall. This track is now followed all the way back to a tarmac road. Turn left and Porth yr Ogof car park is shortly on the right.

'In late autumn the colours of the trees softened here to very unusual hues; and the autumn rains easily convert the Mellte into a really imposing stream, and make these falls even look majestic.'

Ernest Rhys 1911

ROUTE 31
Sgwd Gwladys

4.5km (7.2 miles) and 10 m (98 feet) of ascent

'The Pyrddin has two falls which are among the best in the district, including the Sgwd Gwladys, or Lady's Fall'.

Ernest Rhys 1911

START: Near the Angel Inn at Pontneddfechan where parking is available. GR 901076 (OL12). Toilets and The Waterfalls Information Centre are nearby.

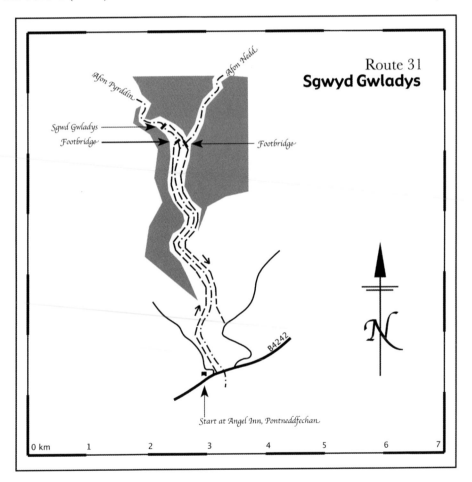

ROUTE DIRECTIONS

(1) On the left of the old stone bridge, follow a path signposted 'Sgwd Gwladus Lady Waterfalls'. It runs beside the western bank of the Afon Nedd and shortly passes a high overhanging sandstone cliff which is known as the 'Farewell Rock'. Such outcrops were given this name by iron-ore miners and colliers around the turn of the eighteenth century because it marked the end of the iron-ore and coal seams.

The broad path is well constructed, for the first kilometre was originally built as a tramroad to convey silica from the mines which can be seen on both sides of the river, to Pont Walby and the Neath Canal.

Silica mining was started in this valley during the early 1920s after William Weston Young (1776-1847) developed a method of manufacturing fire-bricks of very high quality from the Dinas Silica. It is a hard rock containing a high percentage of silicon oxide which gives it a very high melting point. His bricks were used for lining iron and steel making furnaces, lime kilns and domestic fireplaces. They were in great demand and were exported to Europe and America. It is interesting that even today, the word for 'firebrick' in Russia is 'Dinas'.

On the left of the path will be seen the remains of a water-powered mill, and the millstones which once ground corn from surrounding farms have been preserved here.

(2) On reaching the confluence of the Nedd and Pyrddin rivers there is a choice of routes. The first path to the left, beside the Pyrddin leads to a viewing platform from which Sgwd Gwladys may be observed at a distance. If you wish to get closer to this waterfall then cross the metal bridge at the confluence and turn left up a path that follows the right hand bank of the Pyrddin. It climbs gently through the woods and soon you are looking down on a minor fall which does not appear to have been given a name. Further on the sound of Sgwd Gwladys will soon be heard. Make a short detour to the left to reach the base of the fall.

Sgwd Gwladys is sometimes referred to as the Lady's Fall for its Welsh name commemorates one of the reputed twenty-six daughters of Brychan, King of Brycheiniog in the fifth century. In appearance the fall is similar to Sgwd yr Eira, particularly in full flow. It cascades over a jutting ledge and there is a space behind the fall which one can usually reach along a line of 'stepping stones' at the edge of the cliff, but at high water they will be submerged. The pool directly below the fall is called Pwll Cawth (the Lime Pool).

Sgwd Gwladys (The Lady Fall) on the river Pyrddin

(3) **Now return to the main path and follow it up to a rock platform, level with the top of the fall. But make sure that youngsters keep well back from the edge, for the rock can be very slippery when wet.**

Just beyond the fall is a large boulder which was once a well known rocking stone admired by early visitors to the Upper Vale of Neath. Waring wrote: 'Its weight was calculated at 17 tons and it was so delicately poised on the adjacent rock, that a push of the finger would move it, and the writer has cracked nuts, gathered in the neighbourhood coppice, beneath its ponderous, yet gentle vibrations.' In 1850, when the Vale of Neath railway was being constructed, a gang of navies wandered up the Nedd valley and visited the rocking stone which was fairly well known at that time as being a local curiosity. It did not take them long to move the rock off its fulcrum and put an end to this fascinating trick of nature.

The Rocking Stone above Sgwd Gwladys

Further upstream but very difficult to approach is the dramatic waterfall of Sgwd Einon Gam. A cliff on the north side of the Pyrddin makes it necessary to ford the river beyond Sgwd Gwladys and also twice more, to avoid the steep sides of the valley. This route does not follow any distinct path and it should only be undertaken by experienced walkers and those who are prepared to do some wading.

Sgwd Einion Gam on the river Pyrddin is difficult to reach

(4) Return to the metal bridge at the confluence of the Nedd and Pyrddin and cross the wooden bridge over the Nedd to complete a circuit back to Pont Nedd Fechan. Follow the path beside the river, shortly passing the entrance to a Silica mine. In due course you will reach a stile in a fence. Ignore the path signposted to the left and continue along the broad track which runs above the river and then descends past the ruins of an old building.

(5) Cross a footbridge spanning a gully and pause to observe the fascinating remains of man's endeavours, where past industry was once a source of local employment. Then, continue beside the river and soon the track begins to traverse the steep bank on the left. It becomes narrower and winds its way across the steep side of the valley to then descend once more to river level. After passing the entrance to another mine, the path leads on between moss clothed trees to reach a finger post. From here, follow a path to the left, signposted Pontneddfechan. It zig zags up the tree covered hillside to reach a stile in a fence.

(6) Cross the stile and continue beside the fence to another stile. Then walk through an open area, cross a stream on a three-plank bridge and continue beside a fence. The path then descends to a footbridge over a stream. Go left up a stepped bank and turn right to cross a stile in a fence. Continue along a rocky path to shortly cross a stile and pass between a school and a house.

(7) Turn right along a pavement and at a bend in the road (by a bus shelter), turn right and follow a signposted tarmac path which leads down between stone walls to a long flight of steps, and emerges by the old stone bridge in Pontneddfechan.

'At Pont Nedd-Fechan, we are in the bosom of converging hills. Four considerable streams renowned at one time for the height and beauty of their many waterfalls and their weird subterranean journeyings here mingle their waters close at hand.'

A.G. Bradley 1911

ROUTE 32
The Waterfall Roundabout

14 km (8.75miles) and approx 150m (500 feet) of ascent

'To visit the waterfalls in the Vale of Neath, the tourist must make up his mind to a day of toil - to be largely repaid.'

Mr. and Mrs. S.C. Hall, 1841

START: Pontneddfechan, near the Angel Hotel and the Tourist Information Centre GR 901076 (OL12).

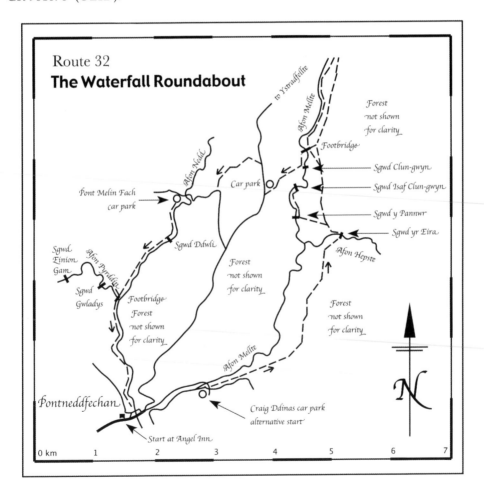

It is a satisfying experience to visit all the main waterfalls in one day but it should be emphasised that this can be a tiring route and should not be attempted by those unused to walking in rough country.

ROUTE DIRECTIONS

(1) **Follow the road to the right (east) to pass the Craig y Ddinas Hotel. Do not follow the road uphill but continue past houses to cross a bridge over the river and reach Craig y Ddinas which is an impressive limestone crag. Now follow a rocky and steeply rising path to the left of the crag with the River Mellte dashing by far below. About an hour of steady walking will bring you to a large prominent boulder directly above the Hepste Gorge and from here the sound of Sgwd yr Eira will be clearly heard.**

(2) **Descend the stepped path with care and then follow a rocky path to pass behind the fall. After a short distance go up a path on the right which leads up a long flight of steps. On reaching the track above, turn left (path signposted Clun-gwyn Isaf and Sgwd y Pannwr). As you walk along the broad track you will be very much aware of the sound of Sgwd yr Eira in the valley below.**

(3) **The track curves around a promontory above the junction of the two valleys and enters the Mellte Valley. In due course another finger post is reached which points the way down to Clung-wyn Isaf and Sgwd y Pannwr. Descend the rocky path to the valley floor and soon Sgwd Y Pannwr will be heard and glimpsed through the trees.**

(4) **From there, continue along the track to reach Sgwd Clun-gwyn Isaf. It is then necessary to return along the same route back to the high level track. On regaining the high level track, turn left to follow the track signposted to Gwaen Hepste. This track curves around the rim of the valley** and provides splendid views while one is ever conscious of the sound of rushing water. In particular the noise made by Sgwd Clun-gwyn Isaf will shortly be heard far below in the depths of this dramatic gorge. Many of the trees appear to be twisted into strange Disney-like shapes and the route is along a waymarked (green) route which takes you along a section of track which has been cobbled with large stones to combat some particularly glutinous mud. **After crossing a stream gully, the path continues around the rim of the valley and then turns left to cross another stream.** Just beyond here is the upper fall which is named Sgwd Clun-gwyn.

(5) **After admiring the fall, return to the upper track and then continue left to reach a footbridge. Cross it and turn left to follow the right hand bank of the Mellte in a southerly direction, and there is now an opportunity to view the last fall from another angle.**

Sgwd Isaf Clun-gwyn on the river Mellte

The Horseshoe Falls on the Nedd Fechan

Sgwd Einon Gam completely frozen is a rare sight

Then follow the path in a south-westerly direction, away from the valley to pass through meadows and past a restored farmhouse. Cross two stiles and follow a broad track up to the Pontneddfechan - Ystradfellte road.

(6) Turn right along the road, and opposite a one-time chapel go up some steps in the bank on the left and cross a stile, (Signposted 'Heol -fawr'). Head directly across the field via stiles to pass through a gate and then turn left along a tarmac lane. Beyond a farm it becomes a muddy track. Go through another gate and bear left to pass beneath trees arching over the wide track which leads on to another gate. Shortly go over a stile on the right of the next gate. Turn right and walk down an ancient lane heading towards the Nedd valley.

(7) Go through a gate just above a farm where several barking dogs may greet you. Turn right and follow the road down to a stone bridge over the river in the bottom of the valley. This is Pont Melin-fach (Small Mill Bridge).

(8) From the picnic site follow the western bank of the river Nedd Fechan to reach the upper and lower Ddwli Falls and later, the Horseshoe Falls which are near a footbridge over a small ravine down which flows a tributary of the Nedd Fechan. The bridge is called Pont Nant Llechau.

(9) Continue along the track through this dramatic gorge and in due course you will reach a metal footbridge at the confluence of the Nedd and the Pyrddin. From the metal bridge follow the right bank of the Pyrddin to visit Sgwd Gwladys and (if prepared to wade) Sgwd Einion Gam. Retrace your steps to the metal bridge and cross it to follow a broad path beside the Nedd back to your starting point at Pontneddfechan.

'I cannot call to mind a single valley that in the same extent of country comprises so much beautiful and picturesque scenery and so many interesting features as the Vale of Neath.'

Alfred Russell Wallace

FFOREST FAWR

'This is a grim inhospitable land, uninhabited and awesome, yet with its own strange perverse beauty.'

Tudor Edwards

Fforest Fawr (Great Forest) can be defined as the area between the A4067 and the A4059 and it includes the summits of Craig Cerrig-gleisiad, Fan Frynach, Fan Fawr, Fan Llia, Fan Nedd, Fan Fraith and Fan Gyhirych.

Many walkers who come here expect to find a dense forest as the name suggests. However, it was never a forest in the normal sense for it was established as a game reserve by Bernard de Newmarch after he had defeated Bleddyn ap Maenarch, the last Welsh ruler of the area. Large herds of deer roamed the hillsides and these were maintained by the Norman lords to provide good hunting. Apart from the sporting interest, it also meant that supplies of fresh venison were readily available during the winter season, to supplement the diet of salted meat obtained from the annual slaughter of domestic animals. Undoubtedly the Forest played an important part in the medieval economy of this area.

The boundary of the Forest followed the main stream of the Usk from its source as far as the River Camlais, then ascended beside that stream to continue over the ridge of Mynydd Illtyd to the River Tarrell, to Storey Arms - there joining the River Taff and on to Nant Pennig and the upper reaches of Nant-yr-Eira. From there it crossed the moorland to reach the western boundary of Brycheiniog on the Twrch. It then continued along the county boundary over the Carmarthen Fans to reach the source of the River Usk. The area was called Fforest Fawr to distinguish it from Fforest Fach on its north side between Cwm Treweryn and the lower Crai valley.

Farmers had pasture rights on Fforest Fawr until the Enclosure Act of 1815-19. During the last century this area of 50 square miles has been used for sheep-rearing on a large scale.

Fforest Fawr culminates in a line of bold summits. They run from the Carmarthen boundary where Bannau Brycheiniog rises to 2,632 feet (802m) and is linked to the escarpment of Fan Hir and eastward to Fan Ghirych, Fan Nedd, Fan Llia and Fan Fawr, (2409 feet). Fan Frynach (2,047 feet) above the Tarell valley, is the highest northern outlier of Fforest Fawr.

In 2005, Fforest Fawr Geopark was designated by the United National Educational, Scientific and Cutural Organisation (UNESCO). It is the only example in Wales and one of five in the United Kingdom.

For more information visit: www.fforestfawrgeopark.org.uk

ROUTE 33
Fan Fawr and Fan Frynach

'The Eric Bartlett Memorial Walk'

12 km (7.5 miles) and 540 m (1,771 feet) of ascent

'The wonderful precipice of Craig Cerrig-gleisiad, with its sheer walls of naked rock some five hundred feet in height, within a stone's throw of the road, strikes a fine note amid solitude.'

A.G. Bradley 1903

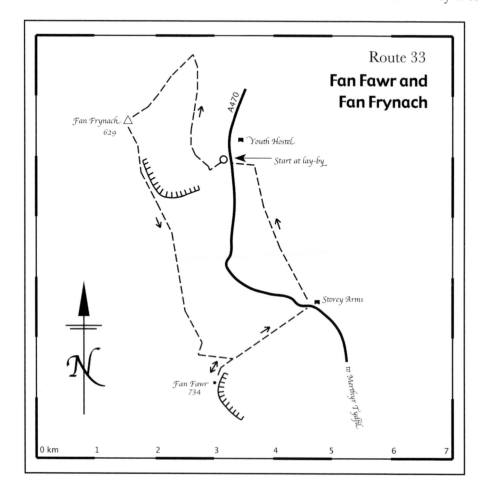

START: From lay by on the A470 about 7 miles south of Brecon and below Craig Cerrig- gleisiad GR 972222 (OL12).

ROUTE DIRECTIONS
(1) **Go over a stile to follow a path which is signposted 'Twyn Dylluan' and 'Forest Lodge'. Keep straight on beside a fence** to shortly pass a stone on the right which bears a plaque inscribed:

'This wood is established in memory of Eric Bartlett
(1920-1986) who did so much for wildlife in the countryside.'

For nearly 30 years Eric Bartlett was the warden of Ty'n y Caeau Youth Hostel, near Brecon, where people from all over the world made his acquaintance. For the next ten years he was employed as a sub-agent by the National Trust. Eric was involved with many different local organisations but he always took a very special interest in the Brecon Beacons National Park. He was a member of the Breconshire Park Planning and Joint Advisory Committee from 1960-1974 and then became a member of the Countryside Committee for Wales. In 1982 the Secretary of State appointed him to the National Park Committee.

Eric had considerable interest in a wide range of countryside matters ranging from natural history to mountain rescue. He also served as a local magistrate for many years. This wise and respected man was well known throughout the area and he sadly died in 1986 at the early age of sixty six.

(2) **Walk on towards the dramatic cliffs of Craig Cerrig-gleisiad 'Blue-stone Rock'). On reaching a gate, squeeze through a slot in the wall on the left and enter Craig Cerrig-gleisiad National Nature Reserve**. It covers an area of 493 hectares and there is a variety of plant life on the crags, including rare arctic-alpine plants, such as purple saxifrage and mossy saxifrage. Trees and shrubs include hawthorn, rowan, mountain ash and rare whitebeams.

Birds to be seen here include ravens, kestrels, skylarks, ring ouzels and meadow pipits.

(3) **Follow a path to the right, keeping a stone wall on your left. Good views may be enjoyed of the craggy ampitheatre to the left and down the valley towards Brecon. The path drops down to cross a stream. Go over a stile to continue, in due course, beside a fence and then a stone wall, ascending gently all the time. The path soon descends to ford another stream and then continues up then the other side**. In the distance now can be seen the distinctive north escarpment of the Black Mountains.

Craig Cerrig-gleisiad National Nature Reserve

View of the Brecon Beacons from summit of Fan Frynach

(4) **In due course, the path leaves the stone wall and rises up above a wood to reach the skyline at a low col. Cross a stile in a fence beside a gate and take in the extensive view to the north. Just beyond the stile is a hairpin bend. Turn left here to follow a broad track heading up towards Fan Frynach**. The ascending path now provides a good view up Glyn Tarrell with the distinctive table-like summit of Pen-y-Fan and Corn Du on the left. The cliffs of Craig Cerrig-gleisiad come into view with Fan Fawr 'towering' above. **Cross a stile beside a gate and continue along the broad track. Shortly make a brief detour to the right to take in the trig' point marking the summit of Fan Frynach (629m).**

(5) **Retrace your steps and continue along the broad track to join a fence and then descend to a col. Just beyond a pool go over a stile beside a gate. A short ascent will bring you to a small cairn on the summit of Craig Cerrig-gleisiad . Keep away from the steep cliffs on the left. Now head south across a wide expanse of moorland following a well trodden path and head for Fan Fawr (Large Peak).**

(6) **One can make a direct ascent of Fan Fawr or head up a short way to reach a path which curves around to the NE slope of the hill where a well trodden route leads up to the high ground above. The trig' point is surprisingly not on the summit but about 0.8 km to the south west (734m).**

(7) **Retrace your steps and descend the north east ridge to follow a path down to Storey Arms**, an Outdoor Activity Centre.

(8) **Cross the road with care and turn left down the old coach route which is now part of the Taff Trail.**

This was once the main turnpike between Brecon and Merthyr Tydfil and used by stage coaches until the present route (A470) on the other side of the valley was constructed in 1830. The old coach road however continued to be used by drovers for many years afterwards.

(9) **After about 2 km a sign is reached pointing the way to Llwyn-y-celyn Youth Hostel. Go over a stile beside a gate and bear slightly left across a field to reach another stile. Follow a path down to a bridge, below which a small waterfall plunges into a pool. Now for the 'sting in the tail' and what will seem the steepest part of this walk. Head straight up the steep field on the other side of the stream to reach a stone stile and the main road. Cross the road with care and turn right to shortly reach the lay by from which you started.**

ROUTE 34
Fan Nedd and Fan Gihirych

24 km (1 miles) and 770m (2525 feet) of ascent

'Fan Frynach and Fan Gyhyrch, Fan Brycheiniog and Fan-hir rolling away behind the other, a confusion of dark rugged masses into Carmarthenshire, made as savage and striking a picture as one could wish for.'

A.G. Bradley 1903

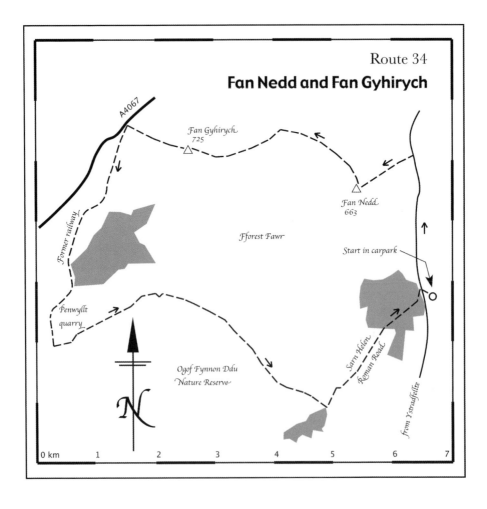

Route 34

Fan Nedd and Fan Gyhirych

A4067

Fan Gyhirych
725

Fan Nedd
663

Fforest Fawr

Start in carpark

Former railway

Penwyllt
quarry

Ogof Fynnon Ddu
Nature Reserve

Sarn Helen
Roman Road

from Ystradfellte

N

0 km   1   2   3   4   5   6   7

This route involves crossing part of the Cnewr Estate which is a large enclosed area of mountain country in private ownership. In 1983 an informal agreement was made between the landowners and the National Park Authority to provide a permissive path across the land, for use on foot by the general public. The Estate and the National Park Authority may agree at any time to restrict access for a reasonable period in respect of fire risk, bad weather, diseases of stock or other cause related to public safety or the safety of the Estate and its livestock.

START: Blaen Llia Car Park GR 927165 (OL12)

ROUTE DIRECTIONS
(1) **Walk up to the road, turn right and follow it in a northerly direction. About 100 metres before reaching the prominent standing stone (Maen Llia), go over a stile in the fence on the left. An ascent of about 234 metres (750 feet) over rough ground leads to the summit of Fan Nedd (Peak of river Nedd) which is marked by a trig' point (663m).**

(2) **Head north towards a cairn and then walk north west down to Bwlch y Duwynt. From here, head west to join a broad track by a gate. It leads up to a col between Fan Gihyrch and Fan Fraith. Continue beside a fence and follow the track to a gateway. Now ascend the slope directly ahead to reach a gate in a fence. Turn left along a gravel track.**

(3) **After about 0.5 km head up the slope on the right and make for the trig point marking the summit of Fan Ghirych (725 m).**

(4) **From here the permissive path shown on the OS map involves a very steep descent from the summit of Fan Ghirych to Bwlch Bryn-rhudd, on the A4067. The majority of walkers tend to avoid this steep, knee-jarring descent by following the ridge southwards to descend a gentler slope and then head north-west to reach a stile at the bwlch.**

(5) **The stile gives access to a layby on the A4067. From here turn left and follow a narrow path leading up the bank on the left below the fence. Shortly, cross a stream flowing down a gully and follow an old railway line.**

This was the Neath-Brecon railway which partly followed the route of the Forest Tramroad and was built in about 1826 by John Christie who purchased part of the Great Forest after the 1819 enclosure. It was used to transport coal and lime from his undertakings at Ystradgynlais.

Maen Llia is a massive prehistoric monolith at the head of the Llia Valley

The Neath-Brecon railway was opened in 1867, was taken over by the Midland Railway in 1877 and later by the GWR in 1923. It was closed to passengers by the famous Dr. Beeching in 1962, but remained open for goods until 7 October 1963.

(6) After about 3 km, the track approaches the hamlet of Penwyllt (Wild Head), a name emenating from its wild and rugged situation. A path rises above the railway and soon you will join a gravel track which passes a quarry on the left and leads to a tarmac road. Now turn left and follow the road to reach a cattle grid and kissing gate. Shortly, the old Penwyllt Railway Station is passed on the right. This is of special interest, having been preserved because it was for many years regularly used by the famous Victorian opera singer Madame Adelina Patti who lived at Craig y Nos Castle. When she died in 1919 her embalmed body was taken from here by train to London and then on to Paris for burial.

Penwyllt used to be a thriving village of about 200 inhabitants. It had a public house (The Stwmp), shop and a post office. One long row of quarrymen's cottages has survived and it serves as a base for the South Wales Caving Club.

(7) From here, follow the path beside a fence around to the right, and just before the long terrace of cottages (Caving Club HQ) turn left up a waymarked path. On reaching a stile, the Ogof Ffynnon Ddu Nature Reserve is entered. This was declared Britain's first cave National Nature Reserve in October 1975 and the area included is both below ground and on the surface.

Ogof Ffynnon Ddu means 'The cave of the Black Spring' and this extensive underground system was discovered in 1946. Birds to be seen in this reserve include peregrine, raven, nightjar, ring ouzel, red grouse, wheatear and red kite.

(8) Just after the stile, bear right. Cross an old incline (constructed to convey silica-sand to the Penwyllt brickworks) and go up the path on the other side. As you ascend the hillside, look out on the right for the gated top entrance to Ogof Ffynnon Ddu cave system. This is about 38 km in length which makes it one of the longest cave systems in Britain, and it is certainly the deepest, involving a total descent of 300 metres.

(9) The track leads on to a stile in a fence and then on across a craggy, boulder strewn hillside. Cross another stile in a fence and make a gentle ascent to join a broader track, which continues over the next rise, and down to a stile in a fence marking the eastern boundary of the Nature Reserve. From here the path leads on through the heather with the Brecon Beacons now in sight.

Sarn Helen

Maen Madoc

The Latin inscription

(10) **After a few kilometres of very pleasant walking, a ruined building will be passed on the left. Shortly join a forestry track and turn right. Go over a stile beside a gate and then turn left through another gate. The wide rutted track leads downhill to reach a ford which can be difficult to cross after heavy rainfall.**

Continuing up the hillside, this ancient track is a Roman road known as Sarn Helen. It was constructed to connect forts at Neath, Coelbren and Y Gaer, near Brecon, and on through Wales to Segontium at Caernarfon. The word sarn means causeway and according to legend the road is named after Elen Luyddawc, a beautiful Welsh princess, who married the Roman General Magnus Maximus (known to the Welsh as Emrys Wledig) in the 4th century. Alternatively, it is considered that Sarn Helen, is really a corruption of Sarn Lleon meaning 'the way of the Legions'.

The gravel track snakes up the hillside and Fan Nedd now looms ahead. Before long the slender standing stone known as Maen Madoc will be seen on the right of the track. It bears a Latin inscription which is now badly weathered and difficult to read but it has been deciphered as:-

DERVAC FILIUS IVST JACIT - 'Dervacus, son of Justus, lies here.'

The identity of Dervacus is obscure and the names do not figure in the genealogies of the royal family of Brycheiniog. The origin of the name Maen Madoc is not known but it is of interest that there is a Castell Madoc about 4 miles due north, near the Senni river and a Nant Madoc about 2 miles further south.

The site was investigated by the Ministry of Works in 1940 and it was decided that the stone had at one time fallen and been re-erected, not in its original position but on the edge of the Roman road. A few feet behind it a large pit was uncovered which may have been the grave of Dervacus.

(11) **The Roman road then passes through a forestry plantation and across the site of a Roman marching camp to join the Ystradfellte - Heol Senni road. Turn right here and return to the car park at Blaen Llia.**

'North eastward of Ystradfellte runs the Sarn Helen, a remote Roman causeway which joins the mountain road above the Afon Llia. Follow this as far as you wish, but do not stray from its course, for this is a grim inhospitable land, uninhabited and awesome, yet with its own strange perverse beauty.'

Tudor Edwards 1950

THE SWANSEA VALLEY

ROUTE 35
Cribarth and the Henryd Falls

14 km (8.75 miles) and 350m (1148 feet) of ascent

'A more romantic habitation than Craig-y-nos would be hard to find, for it lies under the very shadow of the Carmarthen Vans.'

A.G. Bradley 1903

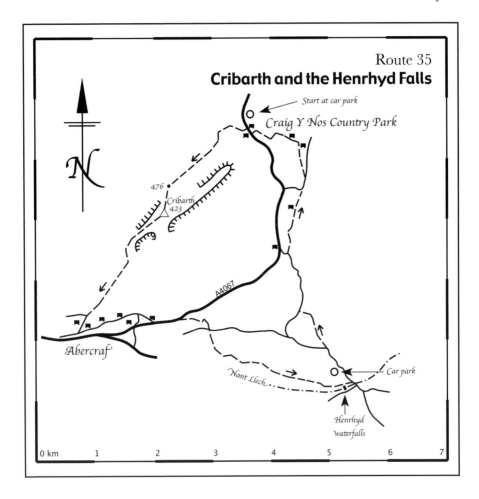

Route 35
Cribarth and the Henrhyd Falls

Start at car park

Craig Y Nos Country Park

476

Cribarth
423

A4067

Abercraf

Nant Llech

Car park

Henrhyd
waterfalls

0 km   1   2   3   4   5   6   7

START: Craig-y-Nos Country Park GR 840155 (OL12) on the Swansea to Sennybridge road (A4067) about 6 miles north of Ystradgynlais. Take note of the time when the Park gates are locked. If there is insufficient time for you to complete the walk then park in a nearby layby on the side of the A4067.

ROUTE DIRECTIONS

(1) About 200 yards south of the entrance to Craig-y-nos Castle, pass through a gap in the stone wall on the right and go over a stile. From here, the track is signposted 'To Open Hill - Tua'r Mynydd'. After 100 yards turn sharp right by a finger post and follow a path up steps. It is marked by white topped posts (at the time of writing) and crosses the hillside to the right, ascending steadily to meet a fence. The path then heads straight up beside the fence.

(2) Where the path divides, the shorter but steeper way is straight on beside the fence. For a more gentle ascent, follow the path to the left (also marked by white topped posts). It curves around the hillside, providing dramatic views of the valley. On meeting a stone wall turn right. Both paths arrive at a ladder stile spanning the stone wall, beyond which is the open hill. Head directly up the hillside to reach more level ground. Pick your way through the limestone outcrops and using sheep tracks and sections of old tramroads, head in a south westerly direction to reach the summit of Cribarth (423m).

This hill was quarried for limestone and rottenstone - which is decomposed limestone and once used as an abrasive for scouring tinplate. The tramroad was built to transport the stone to Abercraf and then on by barge on the Swansea Canal to Ynyscedwyn. There were more than thirty limestone quarries on the summit of Cribarth, no less than eighteen inclined planes and 17km of tramroads and horse-worked railways were built between 1794 and 1895.

(3) Leave the ridge and drop down to a track beside a wall on your left. Follow it down beside the wall and through a little valley to reach a finger post. Cross the stile and keep to the right following a track curving around the hillside. It leads down towards the Swansea Valley, passing a large prominent boulder. On reaching a finger post go over a stile and descend an old industrial incline to reach a stile. Follow a gravel track and at a bend go over a stile and descend the next stage of the old incline. Cross a stile beside a gate and continue down the last section of incline. Go through a kissing gate and follow the road into Abercraf.

Craig y Nos Castle

Cribarth

(4) Turn left and follow the pavement beside the main road. Look out for a tarmac lane on the right opposite Brynseion Chapel. It provides a pleasant alternative to the pavement and leads you down to the river. On reaching a weir, go up a flight of steps and follow a grass path between the fence and the river and beside a childrens' play area. Descend some steps and cross a footbridge; go over a stile and then another footbridge. Continue along this pleasant path until at the end of the fence the path turns left. Cross a stile beside a gate, and turn right along the pavement to shortly reach the Abercrave Inn, where a refreshment stop may be on your agenda.

(5) From the inn, follow the pavement down past the junction with the main road and continue to the left beside the main road, shortly passing Abercrave Outdoor Study Centre. Cross the road and follow the pavement on the other side. By a finger post, opposite St. David's Church, take a gravel track descending on the right. It narrows into a path which leads past cottages to a kissing gate, and then on between fences with pleasant meadows on either side. Continue beside the river to reach another kissing gate and footbridge.

(6) Ignore the path to the right which goes over another footbridge, and keep straight on ascending a flight of wooden steps. Go over a stile and continue along a narrow path above a dingle. Cross a stile, turn right along the road and almost immediately go over a stile on the left. The track now follows the side of a thickly wooded gorge. The cliffs are festooned with ivy and one passes moss covered boulders. The path has now been made safe with steps and handrails but when I first came this way some years ago it was a real expedition. Go over a stile and above a flight of steps the track becomes wider. Ignore the footbridge on the right and shortly pass a ruined building.

The River Llech is a tributary of the Tawe and the densely wooded sides of this ravine are clothed with a wide variety of trees including oak, ash, lime, birch, hazel, alder and wych elm.

(7) Continue through a clearing, ascend more steps and the path now rises above the river again. Cross a stile and a footbridge and the path winds on through the trees up this long and mysterious gorge, which is particularly attractive in the autumn. Soon you are high above the river. Cross a footbridge over a gully and the track continues to snake through the trees. In due course you come to another footbridge spanning a ravine where a stream tumbles down into the gorge.

Henrhyd Waterfall is the tallest in South Wales

(8) The track curves around to ascend a steep slope above the rushing river, then continues through a leafy glade, and still this romantic gorge continues. Descend some steps and the path leads down into the bottom of the gorge to river level for a brief moment and then ascends via rocky steps to reach a path junction. Keep straight on to visit the waterfall. Go down some steps and over a footbridge, then up steps and you enter a craggy ampitheatre at the head of the gorge. The path leads around behind the waterfall, and here you can sit on rocks beneath a big overhang with the water falling before you.

The famous scientist Michael Faraday once came here and later described the scene as follows:-

'Between us and the fall the drops fell brilliant and steady till within a few inches of the bottom, when receiving a new impulse, they flow along horizontally, light and airy as snow. A mist of minute particles arose from the conflicting waters and being driven against the rocks by the wind, clothed them with moisture and created myriads of miniature cascades, which falling on the fragments beneath polished them to a state of extreme slipperiness.'

At 27 metres (90 feet) in height the Henryd Waterfall is the tallest in the National Park. The wooded ravine and falls was acquired by the National Trust in stages between 1947 and 1965.

(9) Retrace your steps to the path junction and ascend the steep path up to the top of the fall. Go through two kissing gates and into a car park. Turn left along a tarmac road which is followed for a short way. Just beyond a mast, go right over a stile and descend to a small footbridge in the bottom of the valley. Cross a field to reach a stile, then cross the next field and follow a fence around to the right. Walk through a gap and continue downhill, keeping the fence on your left and a dingle on the right. The track soon becomes better defined and leads down to a sheep pen. Cross a stile and turn right along a road.

(10) The lane descends past a chapel and after about 400 metres turn right just before a river bridge to follow a tarmac lane which leads to a farm gate. Bear left here along a narrow path running between a hedge and a fence. It then continues as a leafy, tree shaded lane between stone walls. On reaching a road keep straight on and also at the next road junction. Then after about 300 metres take a turning on the left. On reaching a farm ,go through a gate on the left-hand side of the farmyard wall and follow a lane which which later descends beside a moss covered stone wall.

(11) **At a point where the lane rises steeply, follow a track down to the left to reach a hunting gate. Ignore the stepping stones and bridge and turn left over a stile to enter the Craig-y-nos Country Park. Follow the gravel track around to the left and then walk through the trees past a recreation area. Continue beside the river and cross a wide footbridge. Head back to your starting point.**

Craig-y-nos Castle was never really a castle in the true sense of the word and was built in 1842 by the Powell family who sold it to Madame Adelina Patti, a famous opera singer in 1878. She extended the building and even added a 50 seat theatre in 1890 where her guests enjoyed private performances. This 'nightingale' of the Swansea Valley lived here for forty years and during that time she spent a million pounds on the house and grounds. Her staff included 80 servants and 25 gardeners. After her death at the age of 76 on 27 September 1919, her body was embalmed and shipped to Paris where she was buried in the cemetery of Pére Lochaise, Paris, joining the tombs of Chopin and Rossini, to name but a few famous people in the world of music. Craig-y-Nos Castle was purchased in 1919 by the Welsh National Memorial Association for conversion into a tuberculosis sanatorium and it after became a hospital for the elderly. The Castle is now privately owned and is currently being restored to its former glory. Madame Patti's small theatre is in excellent condition and is still used from time to time.

Madam Adelina Patti

THE CARMARTHEN FANS

'Far yonder, are the sharp, shapely peaks of the Camarthen Vans, higher than Plynlimmon at any rate, if not equal to their Breconshire rivals in the Vale of Usk.

A.G. Bradley 1914

The wildest and most remote mountains in the Park lie to the west of the Swansea Valley. They are often referred to as the Black Mountain, which I feel is a confusing name due to the fact that there are Black Mountains on the east side of the Park. Accordingly, I prefer to call this western range the Carmarthen Fans.

These are the most westerly of the Red Sandstone escarpments and provide a five mile line of more or less continuous cliffs facing north and east. They are crossed by few tracks and their wildness and remoteness provides a fascinating attraction for the experienced walker.

West of the main summits of Bannau Brycheiniog and Bannau Sir Gaer are the limestone hills of Carmarthenshire where quarrying has revealed the carboniferous limestone and grit of which these hills are composed. The summits of Carreg-yr-Ogof and Garreg Las with their swallow holes and water worn rocks are not unlike areas of Derbyshire.

It is in this part of the Park that you have the greatest chance of spotting a red kite which a few decades ago was faced with extinction in Britain. As a result of organised protection this strikingly coloured bird of prey, with its distinctive forked tail has made a comeback and sightings of it throughout the Park are becoming quite common. The kite feeding centre at the Cross Inn, Llanddeusant is well worth a visit if you wish to see large numbers of these majestic birds performing aerobatic movements in the sky.

The Red Kite

ROUTE 36
Carmarthen Fans Circuit

21 km (13 miles) 770 m (2525 feet) of ascent

'Their summits (the Fans) are sharp, and the boundary of Brecon and Carmarthen runs through a gorge between them. Their sides are wild and sometimes rocky and broken by shadowy glens that seem to lead into recesses where eerie memories might lurk and the spirit of solitude must surely do so.'

A.G. Bradley 1914

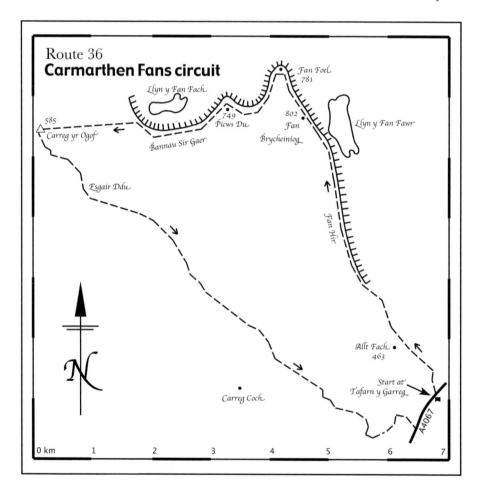

Route 36
Carmarthen Fans circuit

START: Car park at Tafarn y Garreg on side of A4067, GR 848171 (OL12)

ROUTE DIRECTIONS
(1) From the car park follow a signposted path which leads through a gate and then over a wooden footbridge gracefully spanning the river Tawe. Ignore the footpath to the left and continue beside the river for a few hundred metres. Then turn left along a wide track between fences. It leads up to a gate. Now turn right and continue past the end of a large concrete sheep pen and go over a stile to gain access to the open hillside.

(2) Make your way via a long and relentless ascent up the southern end of Fan Hir (Long Beacon) and pick up a path which follows the eastern escarpment. This ridge is about 6.4km (4 miles) in length and provides extensive views across the broad expanse of Fforest Fawr to the Brecon Beacons. A col is reached at Bwlch y Giedd, (where a track known as 'The Staircase' descends to the southern end of the beautiful lake of Llyn y Fan Fawr). From the col ascend to the summit of Bannau Brycheiniog which is marked by a trig' point 802m and a stone shelter which was built in the 1960s.

Llyn y Fan Fawr

(3) **After enjoying the extensive views, continue to the summit of Fan Foel and then turn south west to descend to the col between Bannau Brycheiniog (Breconshire Peak) and Bannau Sir Gaer (Peak of Carmarthenshire). A steep but short climb now leads up to the summit of Bannau Sir Gaer.** It is said to be the highest peak in South West Wales 750m. Bannau Brycheiniog and Bannau Sir Gaer are also known as the 'Horns of Mynydd Du' and they used to stand on either side of the old county boundaries of Breconshire and Carmarthenshire.

Below the steep cliffs of this summit can be seen the mysterious waters of Llyn y Fan Fach which used to be a natural lake, but during World War I it was converted into a reservoir. Llyn y Fan Fach is famous for its legend of 'The Lady of the Lake'. This is the story of a lake maiden who was enticed from the lake by a local farmer. He promised her father, who also resided in the lake, that he would not hit her without cause. Unfortunately he accidently struck her three times and she returned to the lake, taking her dowry of cattle and sheep with her. She later appeared to her sons and told them of healing remedies, and they and their descendants became famous physicians known as the 'Meddygan Myddfai'.

(4) **Continue via Waun Lefrith and then down into the valley and then ascend to the limestone summit of Carreg yr Ogof (585m), which is marked by a trig' point.**This is an area of shattered limestone pavement and the cave from which it takes its name is difficult to find.

The rights of way shown on the map in this area are not so prominent on the ground and accordingly skill with map and compass is essential, particularly in misty conditions. If uncertain about tackling this route, the less experienced walker is advised to return from Carreg yr Ogof via the outward route.

(5) **From Carreg yr Ogof descend in a south easterly direction on a bearing of 130 degrees to reach the Afon Twrch at GR 802197.** This name is associated with the *Mabinogion* story of 'Culhwch and Olwen' and the hunting of a great boar who was pursued across Mynydd Ddu to the Severn. **After crossing the river, make for the summit of Twyn Tal y Ddraenan (GR 809190) and then continue south east to cross the Afon Giedd and on to Pwll y Cig (GR 813184). From here, the track becomes more distinct and continues around the edge of Waun fignen-felin (an area of bog). Beyond Twyn Spratt a broad green track is joined which leads on across wild country to eventually descend into the Swansea Valley near Glyntawe. From there return along the side of the A4067 to your starting point.**

Bannau Sir Gaer

Llyn y Fan Fach

193

ROUTE 37
Fan Foel and Picws Du

12.1km (7 1/2miles) and 610m (2,000 feet) of ascent

'In the distance the mountain rose blue against the moon and the Vans were as sharp and clean as if cut with a knife.'

Richard Vaughan 1951

START: Informal car park at the end of the unclassified road, south east of Llanddeusant, GR 798238 (160).

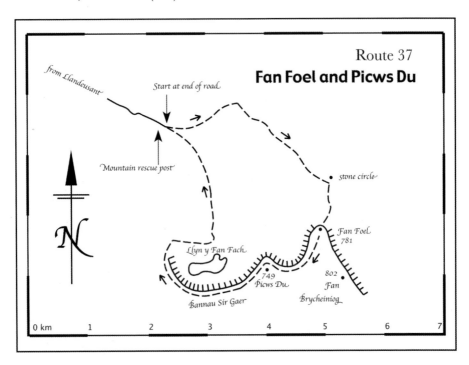

ROUTE DIRECTIONS
(1) **Walk for about 100 yards (91m) in the direction of Llandeusant and then turn sharp right to follow a path contouring in an easterly direction around the hillside. It leads into a little valley formed by the Sychnant stream. Head upwards beside the stream and make for the saddle on the ridge above.**

(2) On gaining the ridge, bear right to follow it, making for the nose of Fan Foel which is now about 1.5 miles (2.4km) away. Climb up a narrow steep path to reach ther summit and then follow the escarpment on the right and steeply down into Bwlch Blaen Twrch.

(3) From the bwlch it is a steep ascent to Picws Du and the summit of Bannau Sir Gaer which is marked by a cairn (2457 feet, 749m).

(4) Follow the edge of the escarpment enjoying the dramatic views and then on via Cwar-du mawr and Cwar-du bach. To the west, the Millstone Grit outcrop of Garreg Las, and the Limestone outcrop of Carreg yr Ogof come into view across the valley of Twrch Fechan. In due course you will meet a path leading down a grassy spur and to the northern side of Llyn y Fan Fach, which is famous for its legendary story of the 'Lady of the Lake' (see Route 36). Until recent years the lake served as a reservoir supplying water to Llanelli.

Llyn y Fan Fach, beneath the dramatic escarpment of Bannau Sir Gaer

(5) On reaching the dam follow the surfaced track which leads downhill past the waterworks filter beds (now used as a salmon and trout hatchery) and back to your starting point.

'The Van Rocks seemed as though near. They rose out of the mountain in their purple and amethyst, and every rain-rut on them caught the gold of the sun.'

Richard Vaughan 1951

ROUTE 38
Circuit of the Usk Reservoir

14 km (7.5 miles) and 260m (852 feet) of ascent

'The head of the Uske river is the Black-mountain, whence it forces its way in a deep channel along a lengthened descent into the Vale. It issues from three apparently inconsiderable springs; but inconsiderable as they may seem, they furnish a constant supply to that noble river, which runs through the heart of Brecknockshire and Monmouthshire and is only surpassed by the Wye'.

H.B. Malkin 1804

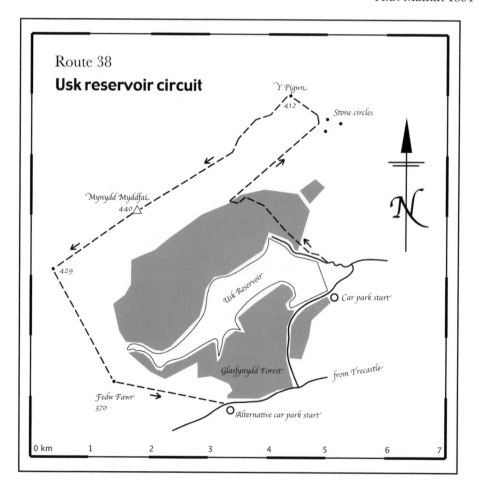

It should be noted that good navigation skills are needed to walk this route in misty weather.

START: Picnic site car park by dam GR 833286 (160)

The Usk Reservoir was completed in 1955 after five years work and opened by the Queen on 6 August of that year. It has a capacity of 2,700 million gallons and supplies water to Swansea.

ROUTE DIRECTIONS
(1) Walk down the road to pass beneath the dam and cross the infant Usk in the bottom of the valley. Turn left at the next junction and continue with the grass covered wall of the dam looming above. Just before reaching the end of the dam, turn right along a tarmac path which changes into a gravel track.

(2) Go through a gate in the corner of the fence and make for a metal hunting gate and then continue to join a broad forestry track which climbs gently through the plantation. Keep straight on at the first forest road junction but shortly, at the next junction leave the road and continue along a grass bridleway.

(3) On reaching a junction of paths turn left to shortly pass a ruined building on the right. About 100 metres further on at a point where the path bends to the left, turn right through the trees to reach a bridleway gate, giving access to the open hillside via a footbridge.

(4) Head towards the skyline to meet the old Roman Road and turn left.
This road was used by the Romans to transport gold mined at Dolaucothi and their camps were built not only to protect this important route but also to provide resting points on the journey.

In the nineteenth century the road was used by stage coaches travelling between London and West Wales. An inn known as the Black Cock used to stand near this spot but it closed in the mid 19th century and there are now no traces of it to be seen.

(5) By a large boulder, head in a northerly direction along a track to reach a grass covered cairn (marked on map) and then 150 metres further on you will reach two prehistoric stone circles situated fairly close together. They date from the Early Bronze Age (around 2000 BC).

The Usk Reservoir

View from Pont ar Wysg

(6) **Just beyond the circles, follow a track which curves around to the left and heads for the NE corner of Y Pigwn fort.** This camp is situated near the highest point of the old Roman road at 412m and was built during the Roman Conquest of 70 AD.

Look back now, and enjoy a view of the Carmarthen Fans, Fforest Fawr, Brecon Beacons, Sugar Loaf and the Black Mountains. This is an excellent vantage point. Looking north, the view includes Mynydd Eppynt and the Cambrian Mountains.

The parallelogram outline of the fort is distinctly visible even though the rampart is very low. Standing here in this lonely spot, one is completely surrounded by mountains and no doubt the Romans found it a wild and inhospitable place.

(7) **Cross the camp and head down to the Roman road. Turn right and continue with the ever brooding Carmarthen Fan to the left. Follow the rutted track around above Cwm-Tan-y-Mynydd and then around the next bend to continue along a grass track to the left, passing below an ancient mound. Then bearing right follow a track towards Mynydd Myddfai.**

(8) **Descend into a col, where there is a junction of tracks. Keep straight on. The round mound on the right is marked on the map as an enclosure. The well rutted track continues steadily upwards. When the main path bends around to the right, keep straight on, heading up hill to reach the trig' point on Mynydd Myddfai (440m).** This also is a splendid viewpoint with the Twi Valley opening up and the Preseli Hills to be seen in the distance.

(9) **Continue along a narrow path following the crest of the ridge. Descend to the next col and then up the other side. The spot height here has been marked by a short concrete post.**

(10) **Now turn left, heading towards Bannau Brycheiniog to join a well trodden path leading across open country to a prominent cairn. Continue, bearing slightly right, but still heading towards Bannau Brycheiniog and looking down on the western end of the reservoir. Now walk in a south-easterly direction over Fedw Fawr and Bryn Pwllygerwn to reach the road at Pont'ar Wysg (Bridge over the Usk).**

(11) **Turn left and cross the bridge to follow the road for about 1 km. Turn left at the next junction and follow road back through the Glasfynydd Forest to your starting point.**

ROUTE 39
Carreg Cennen Castle Circuit

5.5 km (3.4 miles) and 200 m (656 feet) of ascent

'For sheer uncompromising sternness Carreg Cennen has surely no rival in Wales, since here the still imposing remains of an important Norman Castle are perched on a rock some three hundred feet in height and almost precipitous on three sides.'

A.G. Bradley 1904

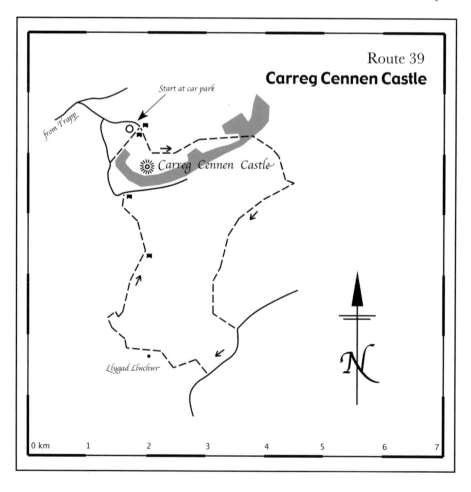

START: Castle car park (with public toilets) GR 666193 (OL12) near the village of Trapp reached by minor roads from A483.

ROUTE DIRECTIONS

(1) **From the public car park walk up the lane to Castell Farm where you may obtain a ticket to visit the castle. Torches can be hired here by those who wish to venture down the underground passage to visit the castle wishing well. However being a sensible and well equipped walker, you will of course already have a torch in your rucksack! Continue to a kissing gate, following the path towards the castle. Go through another kissing gate and along a narrow tarmac path around the base of the castle hillock. A diversion will be made here by those who wish to first visit the castle. Otherwise, carry on to reach a corner, where the view opens out down into the valley below. Bear left and descend a grass path which heads diagonally down the hillside and into the Cennen valley.**

(2) **In the bottom of the valley cross a footbridge over the Afon Cennen. Continue through the trees to reach a stile. Walk on with a babbling stream on the right, which is soon crossed by another footbridge. The path gently ascends beside the stream which now flows in a ravine on the left. Another stile is soon reached. Look back at this point to see the castle perched high on the limestone crag. The path continues, still ascending between high hedges. A flight of steps leads up to a stile.**

(3) **Walk on, now following a cart track around an elbow bend, and at the next junction keep straight on, leaving the main track.** Soon you will reach an excellent viewpoint where a dramatic photograph of the castle may be obtained.

Carreg Cennen Castle is said to be the most romantically situated castle in Wales. It stands on the top of a 330 feet (100 metre) limestone crag above a curve in the River Cennen and is a very dramatic sight particularly when viewed from this direction.

Any enemy who approached the fortress from here would no doubt have quickly come to the conclusion that it was inaccessible. The only way that it could be stormed would be from the northern side where the slopes are not so steep. Alternatively siege tactics could be employed over many months to force the garrison to surrender when on the verge of starvation.

There is a tradition that an earlier castle on this site was occupied by Urien Rheged, Lord of Iscennen, who was said to be one of King Arthur's Knights of the Round Table. Of interest is the fact that for centuries a road running from the castle towards Llandeilo was known as Heol Rheged.

The castle at Carreg Cennen, the sternest, loneliest, rockiest fortress in all that country, rears up its abutments and sheer towers like an Oriental stronghold.'

The present fortress dates from the thirteenth century and it was once the centre of the ancient commote of Is-Cennen, which was part of the Welsh kingdom of Deheubarth South West Wales. Its construction was ordered by the Lord Rhys of Dinefwr, Llandeilo and the castle remained Welsh until 1270. The gatehouse, angle towers and chapel were built in the fourteenth century.

During the revolt of Owain Glyndwr the castle was in the charge of Constable John Skydmore and he held out against the Welsh forces for over a year. Castell Carreg Cennen also saw action during the Wars of the Roses, when it was captured by Lancastrian supporters who later had to surrender to the command of Edward IV. In 1462 five hundred men were employed by the Sheriff of Carmarthenshire to destroy the castle and £28 (in total) was paid to them for undertaking this work.

However, the remains are still very impressive and without doubt the most interesting feature is a corridor passage which leads underground on the edge of the cliff for about 50 metres to a well which supplied water in times of siege.

The corridor passage leads down to a well

(4) **Follow a grass track gently ascending beside a fence. On reaching a stile beside a gate, continue with the fence on your right.**

On the skyline can be seen some large stone cairns. These are prehistoric burial mounds made of rough stones heaped into large piles.

(5) **Continue straight on to reach a gate and the track now becomes better defined. Cross a stile to the right of the next gate and on reaching another stile follow a cart track to reach a stile beside a gate.**

(6) **Turn right now along a tarmac road. Cross a cattle grid and after about 200 yards go right over a stile beside a gate signposted 'Carreg Cennen Circular Walk'. Bear slightly left, walking across a field to reach a stile. Then continue to the left across the next field.**

(7) **The track now broadens and curves down into the valley, where it develops into a stony path, beside a fence and passes below the remains of a lime kiln. A stile on the left gives access to Llygad Llwchwr, a cave at the source of the River Loughor.** It has a very awkward entrance and should only be explored by experienced and properly equipped cavers.

(8) **Go over the stile beside a gate and continue along the broad track beside the river. The path then leaves the river and continues via two stiles.** Carreg Cennen Castle now comes back into view providing another opportunity for dramatic photographs.

(9) **By a fingerpost, follow the track descending to the right. Cross a cattle grid, ford a stream and continue along a gravel track heading directly towards the castle. On reaching Llwyn-bedw farm, don't go through the gate, (Private) but turn left and head straight down a steep field with the castle now looming impressively above you. Go over a stile at the bottom of the field and then bear left down to a footbridge spanning the river Cennen. Cross the next field to reach a stile. Now bear left across the next field to reach a stile giving access to a road.**

(10) **Turn left and follow the steeply ascending road. In due course it flattens out and ahead to the right will be seen the car park / picnic site. Go over a stile on the right and head up through a field towards farm buildings. Here you will find a cafe / shop where refreshments may be obtained. Return to the car park.**

ROUTE 40
Garn Goch Hill Fort

6km (3.75 miles) and 270 m (885 feet) of ascent

'On the opposite side of the valley we see Carn Goch, with its British Camp, and Trichrug, which has the remains of an upstanding cairn on its summit. These peaks rise wild and dark above the leafy barriers of the Vale.'

D. Morgan 1909

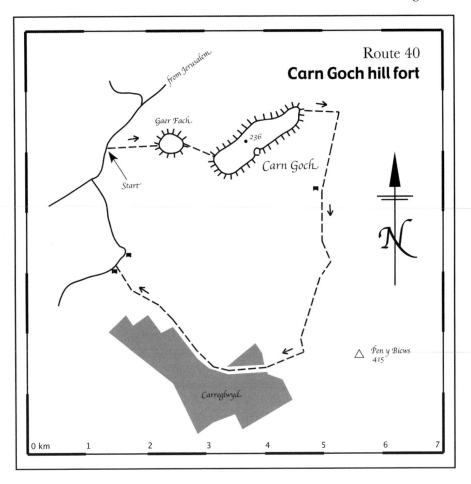

This walk is best undertaken in Spring or Autumn when the bracken is not high, the paths are not obscured and the stone ramparts of the fort can be seen more clearly. The hillside of Garn Goch (Red rocky hill) is owned by the National Park Authority and an information board is positioned on the approach road.

START: at a grass layby near a road junction on the unfenced road leading to Crug Glas Farm GR 682243 (OL12)

ROUTE DIRECTIONS
(1) **Follow a well trodden path up the ridge leading to the summit of Y Gaer Fach (Small Fort)**. From here is an excellent view over the Tywi valley and below can be seen the hamlet of Bethlehem.

(2) **Continue past the outer stone rampart and cross the summit plateau**. Beyond the intervening dip can be seen the large fort of Y Gaer Faw (Big Fort). This is the largest hill fort in Wales, measuring approximately 700 metres by 150 metres. The stone rampart that encircles it has largely collapsed but it is still very impressive on the west side. Follow the path into the dip and up the other side, to ascend a diagonal path which leads up to the impressive hill fort plateau. As you walk across it you will gain an impression of the size of this massive fort. A visit here alone at night is a particularly eerie experience!

Garn Goch is the largest Iron Age hillfort in South Wales

It would seem that there were three phases of construction: an earthen bank which is visible at the eastern end, a massive stone defence wall enclosing 23 acres and an unfinished annexe enclosing a further 9 acres. There were no less than eight entrances with the main one to the east. It had stone towers, a timber bridge and a wooden gate.

(3) **Follow the track through a break in the stone rampart at the far end, and then make your way down, heading towards Tan y Llan farm perched on the hillside opposite. Descend to a road and follow it to the right, ignoring the turning to Tan y Llan farm. After passing through a gate the road becomes a farm track.**

(4) **Shortly leave the track and follow a green lane between hedges. It has been waymarked as a permitted path. Rejoin the farm track and continue through a gate; then on between hedges, gradually ascending to pass a ruined farm.**

(5) **The track ascends the side of Trichrug Hill and at a point where it bends sharply to the left go right over a stile. Then continue along a broad track and go through a gate. Turn right and follow a fence for a short distance to reach a stile. Bear right and cross a stream and an often boggy area. Turn left now beside an old field boundary to pass through a gap in a stone wall. Follow the edge of a wood between a fence and a stone wall to reach a stile in a fence.**

(6) **Carry straight on through a wood following a sunken path beside an old stone wall with your nostrils filled with the scent of pine needles. Windblown trees can sometimes be a problem on this section, although it is clear at the time of writing. In due course, the path descends (follow waymarks) through a more open area to reach a stile. Just below it, cross a track, go left to another stile and cross a stony track. Go left around a stone wall to reach a stile and then on down beside a fence following a wide track through the trees.**

(7) **Cross a stile and go left between a fence and the trees. Continue beside a trickling stream to reach a stile. Keep straight on through the next field and make for a gap in the left hand corner. Now bear left to reach a gate. Walk straight on, keeping a field boundary on the right. Head towards a cottage and then bear left down to a gate. Turn right along a road and on reaching a T junction, turn right (signposted 'Bethlehem') and then bear right again to return to the parking area.**

'The Early Iron Age hill fort of Garn Goch, or the Red Mount, is so called because of the bronze-coloured bracken which distinguishes it in the autumn and perhaps also because of the Old Red Sandstone hill on which it stands.'

Edmund Mason 1975

GENERAL INFORMATION

National Park Information Centres

Abergavenny, Bus Station	Tel: 01873 853254
Mountain Centre, near Libanus, Brecon	Tel: 01874 623366
Brecon Cattle Market Car Park	Tel: 01874 622485
Llandovery, King's Road	Tel: 01550 720693
Pontneddfechan	Tel:01639 721795

Community Managed Information Points

Crickhowell Resource & Information Centre	Tel: 01873 811970
Hay-on-Wye Tourist Information Bureau	Tel: 01497 820144
Talgarth	
	Tel:01874 712226

Special Attractions

Abergavenny Castle and Museum	Tel: 01873 856114
Brecknock Museum	Tel: 01874 624121
Brecon Mountain Railway	Tel: 01685 722988
Castell Carreg Cennen	Tel: 01558 822291
Craig y Nos Country Park	Tel: 01639 730395
Cyfarthfa Castle Museum	Tel: 01685 723112
Garwnant Visitor Centre	Tel: 01685 723060
Goytre Wharf	Tel: 01873 881069
Howell Harris Museum	Tel: 01874 711423
National Showcaves Centre	Tel: 01639 730284
Red Kite Feeding Station, Llanddeusant	Tel: 01550 740617
Tretower Court and Castle	Tel: 01874 730279

Useful Web Sites

Brecon Beacons National Park Authority: www.breconbeacons.org
Brecon Beacons Park Society: www.breconbeaconsparksociety.org
Black Mountain Red Kite Feeding Station: www.redkiteswales.co.uk
Brecon Beacons National Park Authority: www.visitbreconbeacons.com
Brecon Mountain Railway: www.breconmountainrailway.co.uk
Blaenavon Heritage Site: www.world-heritage-blaenavon.org.uk
Cordell Country: www.cordellcountry.org/cordell.html

YOUTH HOSTELS

Dan y Wenallt GR 108205 (160) ia a converted farmhouse pleasantly situated below the Talybont Reservoir. It is ideal for groups and families with a full catering service provided. Tel: 0870 7706136.
Address: Dan y Wenallt, Talybont-on-Usk, Brecon, Powys LD3 7YS.

Llanddeusant GR 776245 (160) is an old inn situated 7 miles south of Llandovery. It feels remote and is well placed for walks in the Carmarthen Fans. There is accommodation for 26 people.
Address: Youth Hostel, The Old Red Lion Inn, Llanddeusant, Llangadog, Carmarthenshire SA19 6UL. Tel: 0870 7705930

Llwyn-y-Celyn GR 973225 (160) is situated 6 miles from Brecon below the A470. It is a traditional Welsh farmhouse with a good atmosphere and is well placed for walks in the Brecon Beacons and Fforest Fawr. There are 42 beds.
Address: Youth Hostel, Libanus, Brecon, Powys LD3 8NH. Tel: 0870 7705936.

Tyn-y-caeau GR 074388 (160) is a fine country house about 3 miles east of Brecon providing comfortable accommodation for 54 people. It is situated between the Brecon Beacons and the Black Mountains in the Vale of Usk.
Address: Youth Hostel, Groesffordd, Brecon, Powys LD3 7SW. Tel: 0870 7705718.

Visit: www.yha.org.uk/find-accommodation/wales/hostels

CAMPING SITES

Llanwenarth Citra, Abergavenny
Pyscodlyn Farm (01873 853271) April - October
www.pyscodlyncaravanpark.com

Brecon
Brynich Caravan Park (01874 623325)
www.brynich.co.uk

Bronllys
Anchorage Caravan Park (01874 711246)
www.anchoragecp.co.uk

Llanddeusant
Black Mountain Caravan & Camping Park (01550 740217)
www.blackmountainholidays.co.uk

Llandovery
Erwion Caravan and Camoing Park (01550 720332)
www.erwlon.co.uk

Llangorse
Lakeside Caravan and Camping Park (01874 658226)
www.llangorselake.co.uk

Pencelli
Pencelli Castle Caravan and Camoing Park (01874 665451)
www.pencelli-castle.co.uk

These are just a few suggested sites and up to date information on others can be obtained from National Park Information Centres. To camp anywhere in the Brecon Beacons National Park requires the permission of the landowner - this includes areas of open land. Special byelaws prohibit camping on National Trust land.

LONG DISTANCE TRAILS
IN THE BRECON BEACONS NATIONAL PARK

Beacons Way
The Beacons Way is a 100 mile walking trail through some of the most varied and beautiful upland landscapes in Great Britain. Designed for experienced wealkers it can be completed over eight consecutive days or explored as a series of linear walks. The route crosses th entire length of the Brecon Beacons National Park
For further information visit: www.breconbeaconsparksociety.org

Cambrian Way
Although not an officially recognised National Trail, this route is described in several guide books and there are numerous variations. Tony Drake of Gloucester was the originator and his route starts in Cardiff and continues via Risca, Twmbarlwm and Mynydd Maen to Pontypool, beyond which it enters the Park. It follows the ridge via Garn Wen to Blorenge and then includes a horse-shoe shaped route in the Black Mountains. From there it crosses the Usk Valley to the Brecon Beacons, to continue over Fforest Fawr and the Carmarthen Fans. It then leaves the Park and heads north over Plynlimmon, Cadair Idris, the Rhinogs, the Snowdon Massif and the Carneddau to finish at Conwy on the North Wales coast. Total Distance 440 km (274 miles). It exceeds the Pennine Way in length by 38 km (24 miles) and involves a total ascent of 18,779 metres (61,540 feet). The average time taken to complete the route is 22 days. Visit: www.cambrianway.org.uk